THE BAFFLED PARENT'S
GUIDE TO
Coaching Youth
SOFTBALL

Jacquie Joseph

Head Coach, Michigan State University

With Lauri Berkenkamp, Nomad Communications
Norwich, Vermont

Ragged Mountain Press / McGraw-Hill

Camden, Maine • New York • Chicago • San Francisco • Lisbon • London
• Madrid • Mexico City • Milan • Montreal • New Delhi • San Juan
• Seoul • Singapore • Sydney • Toronto

To my daughter Emma—for teaching me what is truly important in life.

Ragged Mountain Press
A Division of The **McGraw·Hill** Companies

10 9 8 7 6 5 4 3 2 1

Library of Congress Cataloging-in-Publication Data
Joseph, Jacquie, 1962–
    The baffled parent's guide to coaching youth softball / Jacquie Joseph.
       p.   cm.
    Includes index.
    ISBN 0-07-136825-6
       1. Softball for children—Coaching. 2. Youth league softball—Coaching. I. Title.

  GV881.4.C6 J66 2001
  796.357′8—dc21   00-045892

Questions regarding the content of this book should be addressed to
Ragged Mountain Press
P.O. Box 220
Camden, ME 04843
www.raggedmountainpress.com

Questions regarding the ordering of this book should be addressed to
The McGraw-Hill Companies
Customer Service Department
P.O. Box 547
Blacklick, OH 43004
Retail customers: 1-800-262-4729
Bookstores: 1-800-722-4726

This book is printed on 70# Citation by Quebecor Printing, Fairfield, PA
Design by Carol Gillette
All photographs by Jeff Garland
Production by Nancy Benner and Dan Kirchoff
Edited by Tom McCarthy and Jane M. Curran

Contents

Part One

Coaching 101: The Coach's Start-Up Kit

Preface: Play Ball!

By today's standards, I think I'm an unusual example of someone who has made coaching sports her career. I didn't play competitive sports or even organized sports as a kid. It wasn't until high school that I played any kind of organized sports at all.

I grew up in a city neighborhood with lots of kids. We played street baseball or whiffle ball on someone's driveway or we'd go over to the park and play ball using trees as bases. We had few gloves and just played for fun. My fondest memories of the sport are those when I played catch in my front yard with my dad, my brother, or occasionally my sister, playing hotbox or pickle. I think the reason I became an outfielder was because the only kind of balls my dad could hit were bombs—towering fly balls. It would take three kids just to relay it back to him. I fielded mostly fly balls, so I got pretty good at judging them.

The first day of high school was the first day I played organized sports. A friend of mine encouraged me to try out for the basketball team, so I did. Later in the year, when softball came around, I tried out for that, too. I became an outfielder on the varsity team as a freshman, and played outfield throughout my high school and college years. I also played each summer for a competitive Women's Major team. I played basketball and volleyball throughout high school, but softball was always my favorite.

One of the reasons I wanted to become a coach is that I really loved the game of fast-pitch softball. I enjoyed competition at a high level—I'm very competitive anyway. But the most important motivation was that I was lucky enough to have great coaches who made a huge impact on me. My first softball coach in high school was good and my college coach was exceptional. When I finished playing college ball, she asked if I would stay and coach with her, and I thought if I could give to other players the kind of experience she had given me, I would really be giving something back. I had a wonderful time as a player—we were successful, I learned a lot, and grew as a person and a player, which opened up other opportunities. I wanted to return that gift.

People often ask coaches what their greatest moment as a coach has been. I don't think my best moment as a coach has happened yet. I have

already had many great moments and experiences in the sport, and they've all been different. I won a collegiate conference championship as a head coach, which was great fun. But there are other moments that have been rewarding. I've had kids on my team who really weren't interested in school at first, and to watch them get involved over time with academic pursuits and become excited about graduating is a very special thing to be part of. I also really enjoy the day-to-day interactions with my players. I enjoy helping them get through tough times and come out for the better on the other side.

I get a kick out of the other projects and activities I've been involved with—this book, for example—that I hope will help bring the game of softball to life for other people. There are so many great results when girls have opportunities in sports, and fast-pitch softball is a great one.

I hope that there will be more championships ahead. I hope my greatest moment is yet to come, but championships alone won't be my only measuring stick of success.

Introduction: So You Said You'd Be the Coach, Huh?

So you're a baffled parent.

You were delighted when your daughter told you she wanted to play softball, and you happily drove her to the league signup. But then you discovered that her team didn't actually have a coach, so in a moment of weakness you volunteered. It's been years since you threw anything but a party, much less played softball, and now you're The Coach. Panic is setting in.

Don't worry, help is here. This book is designed to help any coach have a successful season—which doesn't necessarily mean more wins than losses. The advice, games, and drills I provide in this book are aimed at helping you teach 6- to 12-year-olds the basics of softball, sportsmanship, teamwork, and, above all else, the fun and rewards of the game.

Some of the kids you'll be coaching will never have held a softball; others will know more about the game than you do. Some will be aggressive on the field, while others would rather sit on the bench. Some players will be in it for the social aspects, while others will concentrate on the competitive nature of the game. All your players, however, will want to enjoy what they are doing, experience being part of a team, improve their skills, and have fun. These, and many others, are challenges I deal with throughout the book.

How to Use This Book

The Baffled Parent's Guide to Coaching Youth Softball is organized so that you can read it straight through, or you can pick and choose the sections most useful to you at any time. It provides advice on everything from the philosophy of the game to the nuts and bolts of creating a lineup. It also contains a system of individual technique and skill development, from the basics to more advanced skills, complete with an independent section devoted entirely to drills and clear illustrations to guide you every step of the way.

Part 1, Coaching 101: The Coach's Start-Up Kit, will introduce you to the game and take you through the season on a step-by-step basis. Worried about how to establish yourself as the coach in a positive manner? Chapter 1, Creating an Atmosphere of Good Habits, will help you. Do you need to brush up (or learn) the basics of the game? Chapter 2, Before Hitting the Field: Softball in a Nutshell, will give you an overview of the entire game, from where your players should be on the field to how many outs in an inning. If your biggest worry is the administrative end of coaching a youth team, check out chapter 3, Setting up the Season. To learn all about the fundamentals of playing and coaching softball, turn to chapter 4, Essential Skills—and How to Teach Them. Chapters 5 and 6 will help you design practices, assign positions, and develop a practice schedule. For advice about game day, read chapter 7, Game Time. Chapter 8, Dealing with Parents and Gender Issues, offers advice about how best to work with parents and any gender issues that may arise during the season.

Part 2, Drills: The Foundation for Development, Success, Happiness, and a Coach's Peace of Mind, is a coach's dream—a reservoir of drills for all aspects of the game, from batting and pitching to team offense and defense. First mentioned in chapter 4, the drills in part 2 are explained in greater detail. They are also broken down into offense and defense for further clarity. I recommend first trying the drills as I've explained them and then modifying them to fit your own team—just as no two kids are exactly alike, no teams will be the same, either. The drills are designed to be as flexible as you need them to be.

Drills are divided into three areas: warm-up (W), defense fundamentals (D), and batting practice (B). The baserunning drills in chapter 9 and the Controlled Fungo drill in chapter 10 are also appropriate as ending activities. Drills are numbered consecutively by type and are assigned a difficulty level. An *easy* drill is appropriate for a beginning player; there are no prerequisites. An *intermediate* drill assumes that the player has mastered elementary skills and has learned some basic softball terminology. A drill labeled *advanced*—and there aren't many in the book—assumes the player has had game experience and is familiar enough with the game to perform the technique or drill. All drills are designated easy unless otherwise noted. Most, if not all, drills can and should be used for all levels—the techniques used are the same at every level; you will simply modify the repetitions and your performance expectations.

Questions and Answers sections throughout the book address common and hard-to-handle issues, and sidebars are designed to encourage you and provide a little more information on a topic discussed in the text. Photos illustrating many of the concepts covered in the text are included in every section as well. An appendix with Umpire Signals, a sample page from a scorebook, a glossary, and a resources section round out the information. A detailed index helps you find what you need when you need it.

A Word on Coaching

This book is meant to be used as a reference and a guide. The advice I give on these pages is what works for me. Every coach is different in style, temperament, and skill, but we all should have one common goal: to help the kids we coach to get the most out of their sports experience.

I inherently believe that kids want to be good, want to be stars, and want to be successful. I believe you can have high expectations and be demanding in performance—and receive a great deal from your players simply by coaching with positive support and encouragement. Kids naturally strive to do well and respond better to positive encouragement—they feel more empowered and become more independent if they expect more of themselves. I feel there is no place in youth sports for tearing down a player—it wouldn't have worked on me, and I don't believe it will work on yours, either.

Remind yourself that your goal is to provide a fun and rewarding softball experience for your players. This is an opportunity for you to make a difference in their lives, and the lessons they learn now will carry over to life outside of sports. Working together, you and they have the opportunity to learn about the game, enhance softball skills, and experience the fun and excitement of becoming a team.

There are five keys to being a good coach:

Care about your players. Come to the role of coach with a genuine concern for the players and be committed to helping them have a good experience and get better at the game. I have seen coaches with lots of sports knowledge who didn't have genuine concern for players and the notion of a team, and it affected the kids' enjoyment of their experience in a negative way.

Be credible. Learn the basics of the game before you head out on the field. If you don't know what you're doing, the kids will pick up on that and won't respect you. You don't need to be an expert on the intricacies—at the youth level, a solid knowledge of the basics is fine. Learn the basics, learn the rules, and be prepared.

Be authentic. You need to be comfortable with who you are and coach to your personality. Certainly you can learn from other coaches, but you need to be comfortable with your own style. Keep the game fun and have your players trust you—this will happen if you're true to yourself.

Keep it fun. The number one reason kids get out of sports is that they're no longer having fun. Usually this happens when their skills aren't improving. You'll have some players who are much more skilled than others and who will be enjoying what they do more—but you don't have to be a highly skilled player to be successful. If you can help the kids to stay focused on what they do well and to work on improving what they need to work on, without dwelling on what they haven't mastered, they'll have a lot of fun, improve their skills, and stay in the game longer.

Remember your audience. There are differences in how kids respond to their sports experience: some kids are in sports for the social reasons as much as anything else. That's not necessarily bad, but it means you need to allow players time for the social aspect of being on a team as well as developing their softball skills.

Note: The information and advice in this book apply equally to boys and girls. Since predominantly girls play softball at the youth level, I have chosen to use the feminine pronoun throughout this book. Coaches should be aware, however, that in October 2000 the Little League Baseball International Board of Directors approved the worldwide implementation of a Boys Softball Division for players ages 5–18 in 2001.

Sandwich Method of Constructive Criticism

A good way to provide constructive criticism in an effective way is to use the sandwich method: comment on something your player does well, sandwich in some constructive criticism, and then end the conversation with another comment about something she's doing well. She'll feel good about what she can already do, and be excited about working to improve the skills at which she is less accomplished.

Coaching 101:
The Coach's Start-Up Kit

CHAPTER 1

Creating an Atmosphere of Good Habits

One of the most important jobs you'll have as a coach is to help instill good habits in your players. The best way to do this is to set a good example for them to emulate. Although this may be the first time you've ever coached, walk into practice on Day One projecting confidence, whether you feel confident or not. Kids will look to you for knowledge and discipline, they'll expect you to help them develop the confidence they need to push themselves, and they'll take their cues from you. If you walk into your first practice or team meeting and you're unsure of yourself, your players will pick up on that, and you'll have a more difficult time earning their respect. Carry yourself like you know what you're doing. You certainly don't have to know the answer to every question they'll ask—but be firm about when you'll get back to them with an answer. If you are fearful or unsure of yourself, kids will pick up on that—and you're doomed. Come in confident!

Establish Your Identity as Coach

Your players need to know what to call you—you may be coaching your own children, your neighbor's kids, or kids you've never met. Whether you prefer to be called "Coach," your first or last name, or a nickname, make

As coach, you're the team leader. Work early to establish that identity.

sure that during practices and games everyone calls you that name all the time, including players, parents, and your assistants. This helps reinforce your role as the leader of the team. Umpires should always call you "Coach," and you should call umpires "Ump" or "Blue."

Maintain Routines

Kids thrive on routine—they like the certainty of knowing what's expected of them as soon as they step on the field. Routines also pave the way for good habits. On the first day of practice, establish a routine for the practice time, go over it with your players, and stick with it

Encourage your players to look out for one another— you'll see the results quickly.

throughout the season. It can be as simple as everyone gathering at the beginning of the session for a quick meeting and cheer, or jogging and stretching together for a warm-up. The important thing is to be consistent—start and end every practice the same way, every time, throughout the season.

Positive Peer Pressure Is Effective

Peer pressure is a powerful tool that you can use to your advantage. One of the keys of creating good habits and a strong team is to get your players to think of themselves as "we" rather than "I." One thing I require of all of my players is that they show respect for the team by looking like a team even at practice—all players have to be neat in their appearance. This promotes the power of a team, not the individual. Encourage your players to look out for the other players on the team; everyone should take some responsibility regarding the team's welfare.

Be Patient and Positive

Regardless of the age group you coach, you should always start with the basics and be patient with yourself and your players. Don't ever assume kids have any knowledge at all—and remember that what they think they know may not be accurate. You may need to repeat the same thing many times— young players, especially, often need to hear the same things over and over before they "get it." Keep everything you say positive; remember that the

Let Your Signal Be Their Guide

At the beginning of the very first day of practice, stand just outside the third-base line and call "Everybody up!" The kids, who'll be throwing and catching with one another or looking for bats and gloves, will straggle in one by one without much hustle or enthusiasm. After they all finally gather, let them know that when you call the team together, you expect an immediate response of sprinting to you. But tell them that they get another try. Send them back to where they were and to what they were doing before you called them. Call "Everybody up!" again. If they do not respond in the way you've explained, do it again until every player comes to the circle immediately. When the team gets it right, reinforce that with enthusiasm. Let them know that they're working like a team and have them acknowledge it, too, by high-fiving with their gloves.

key to improvement is being willing to fail, and that taking athletic risks can be intimidating for children. Keep your explanations brief, keep your constructive criticism positive, and keep the energy level high. Everyone will enjoy the time you spend together much more.

Drills to Promote Teamwork

Around-the-Horn Throwing W4

This is a good drill to promote teamwork, and it can be done any time during practice. The goal of the drill is to inspire your players to achieve as many successful throws from player to player around the bases as possible. Every player on the team participates in the drill, and players count together as each successful throw is completed. At each practice inspire your players to achieve a new record number of throws or set a new goal for them to try to meet. If they do meet it, celebrate their achievement. If they don't, applaud their efforts and encourage them for next time. (See drill W4 on pages 89–90.)

Every game has a winner and a loser. Teach your players to play each role graciously.

Questions and Answers

Q. I have 18 kids on my team. How do I deal with this large number?

A. Softball is a team game that is learned primarily on an individual basis. Most of the time at practice your players will be learning individual skills that won't make large numbers a problem. However, when you do perform team drills and drills in which players are set at their positions, distribute the kids evenly among the positions. By practicing this way, you and the kids will become accustomed to sharing positions with teammates and, in addition, to sharing playing time come game day. Remember that if you have a large number of players, team discipline and your organizational skills will matter even more than usual (see Appropriate Numbers of Players on the Team on page 26).

Q. I have a player who is consistently late to practice, but it's not her fault. Her parents are late in bringing her. How do I deal with the situation?

A. If there is another family who would be willing to carpool, suggest to the player's parents that they work out an arrangement so that one family is bringing the players to practice and another is taking them home. You can't control the parents' behavior, and it isn't the player's fault, so at this level you'll probably have to grin and bear it.

Q. I have a player on my team who is there only because her parents have forced her to play. She is constantly talking while I'm talking and is quite disrespectful. What do I do?

A. Many times kids seek out negative attention because it's better than no attention at all. Bring her aside one day and talk to her about her behavior, stressing how much you want her there but only if she can be a part of the team, not a drag on it. Some kids respond especially well if given a special job that is just for them, such as being in charge of the equipment or helping to set up the stations for batting practice. If the situation persists, though, you'll need to talk to her parents and make a mutual decision to either keep her on the team or not.

Teaching Your Players to Be Good Sports

Kids are inherently competitive—they like to know what the score is, who won, and by how much. Wins and losses are part of competition, and doing both with grace is a learned skill. Just as you'll help your players develop their softball skills, you can also help them learn to take winning and losing in stride. Include small competitions within the framework of your practices, so your players learn to experience winning and losing—and how to handle both—before they get into a game situation.

Good Players Make Good Friends

One of the most important benefits I've gotten from playing sports has been the friendships I've made throughout the years. I still see people I met and made friends with in my earliest days of playing, and I certainly remember the travel and the friends and coaches I met along the way much more than the wins and losses. I've gained some of the best friends I've ever had and the finest people I've ever known through sports.

Q. As the season has progressed, my team takes longer and longer to gather together at the start of practice when I call "Everybody up!" I now need to yell at them in an angry tone to get a response. How do I regain control?

A. Go back to the beginning. Call them in and reinforce once again the importance of listening to you. If they continue to give you trouble, send them out again and try it again until they get it right. Do not begin practice until you are satisfied with their response to your call. You are the leader and the one responsible for teaching and enforcing good habits and proper behavior. Finally, when they do get it, reward their efforts with genuine positive reinforcement. Begin practice and, unless the problem arises again, leave the situation behind you.

Q. The disparity in ability on my team has led to the better kids picking on less talented kids out of frustration. I can understand their frustration, but it is ruining the team atmosphere. What should I do?

A. You need to make it perfectly clear that there is no place on your team for negative comments about any player by any player, ever. This is a nonnegotiable rule. Take aside the kids who are good and tell them that because they are gifted, they have a responsibility to help the less-skilled players. Stimulate the better kids—pair them up for some of the drills and give them bigger challenges. Also, some players who are more skilled won't throw hard to a less-skilled player because they're afraid of hurting this player. Keep the skilled players together so they challenge each other. Keep them motivated.

If the problem persists, talk to the parents of the more-skilled players. There are very competitive leagues in most cities, and if that's what one or several of your players are looking for, perhaps that is a better place for them.

Before Hitting the Field: Softball in a Nutshell

Softball is a game of quick bursts of action and periods of waiting, but in those waiting periods there is a lot to think about. And for the coach, there is hardly enough time to think about all that you should in between the action. This chapter is an overview designed to introduce you to the basics of softball, including important rules, positioning, and even what to think about between pitches. More specific advice and strategy will come in later chapters, but this should get you started in the right direction.

Basic Rules and Positioning

Softball and baseball are unique in that they are the only sports where the defense has the ball. Specifically, there are nine players playing on defense at any one time in the following positions (see diagrams page 12).

Infield (IF)

Pitcher: positioned on the pitcher's plate or rubber in the middle of the infield.
Catcher: crouches behind home plate.
First-Base Player: positioned a few steps in front of first base.
Second-Base Player: positioned between first and second base.
Shortstop: positioned between second and third base.
Third-Base Player: positioned a few steps in front of third base.

Outfield (OF)

Left Fielder: positioned in the outfield so that the player views the batter between the shortstop and third-base player (distance away from home plate for all outfielders depends on the potential power of the batter and thus will vary).
Center Fielder: positioned in the outfield behind second base.

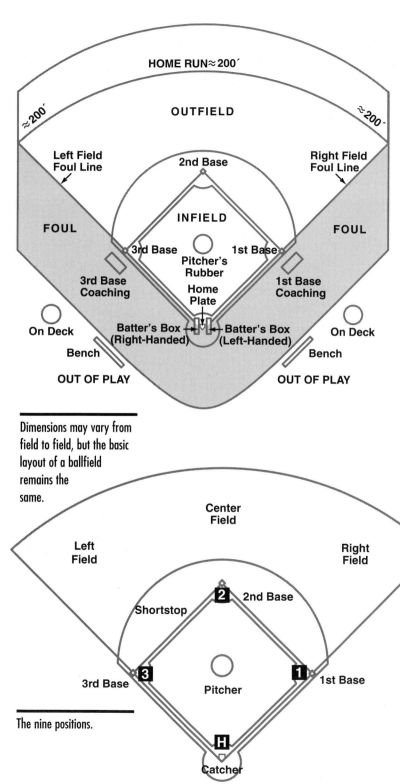

HOME RUN≈ 200´

≈200´

OUTFIELD

≈200´

Left Field
Foul Line

2nd Base

Right Field
Foul Line

INFIELD

FOUL

FOUL

3rd Base

1st Base

Pitcher's
Rubber

3rd Base
Coaching

1st Base
Coaching

Home
Plate

On Deck

Batter's Box
(Right-Handed)

Batter's Box
(Left-Handed)

On Deck

Bench

Bench

OUT OF PLAY

OUT OF PLAY

Dimensions may vary from field to field, but the basic layout of a ballfield remains the same.

Center
Field

Left
Field

Right
Field

2 2nd Base

Shortstop

3 3rd Base

1 1st Base

Pitcher

H

Catcher

The nine positions.

Right Fielder: positioned in the outfield so that the player views the batter between the first-base and second-base players.

The Softball Field

Most fields will vary in their outfield dimensions; some will have fences and some will not. But what do not change are the distances between the bases and between the pitching rubber and home plate. The distance between the bases on a youth league field is 60 feet, and the distance between the rubber and home plate is 36–40 feet (league rules prevail).

Innings and the Object of the Game

Games for older players last seven innings, but in most youth leagues 6- to 12-year-olds play up to five innings. An inning begins with the "top" half and ends with the "bottom" half. The visiting or "away" team bats in the top half of the inning, and the "home" team bats in the bottom half of the inning. The object of the game is to score more runs than the other team, and runs can be scored only when your team is at bat. Runs are scored by touching home plate after safely reaching all three bases. Defensively, the goal is to keep your opponent from scoring runs. A half-inning changes from the top to the bottom after three outs are made by the defense.

Start of an Inning

As the pitcher warms up her arm by throwing to the catcher, the first-base player warms up the other infielders by throwing ground balls to them, and the outfielders throw fly balls back and forth or play catch with other, non-starting players on the foul line. When the pitcher feels loose and ready, usually after five pitches, and the umpire signals play, the pitcher throws to the batter in an attempt to get her out, and the game is under way.

The Strike Zone and the Count

The strike zone varies for each batter, depending on her size. The zone is as wide as home plate (17 inches) and extends vertically from the bottom of the batter's kneecaps to below her armpits. If the batter swings at the pitch and misses, it is automatically called a *strike*. If the batter does not swing, and the pitch is thrown outside of the strike zone, it is called a *ball*. If the pitch does cross through the zone, it is a *strike*. These calls are dependent on the judgment of the umpire, who "calls 'em as she (or he) sees 'em." Each batter receives a *count* of the number of balls and strikes. If the pitcher throws four balls it is called a *base on balls*, or a *walk*. If the pitcher throws three strikes, the batter is *out*. If the batter hits a *foul ball*, which means a hit that does not land within the foul lines, or baselines, it is considered a strike (unless there are already two strikes, in which case it does not affect the count). If a foul ball is caught in the air by one of the players on the field, the batter is out. A ball hit between the baselines is a *fair ball* and must be fielded by the defense.

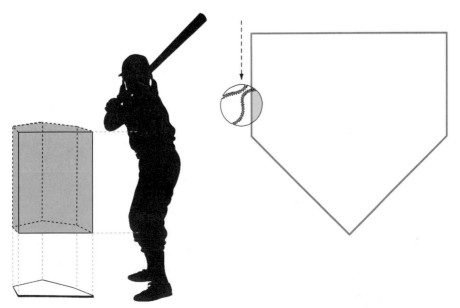

The strike zone. The rulebook strike zone is from the knees to below the armpit (left). Any part of the ball thrown over any part of the plate is a strike (right).

The Ball Is in Play

A batted ball can result in either the batter reaching base safely or being called out by the umpire.

How a Batter Makes an Out

In addition to striking out, a batter can make an out either by grounding out or flying out. A *ground out* refers to a batted ball that is fielded off of the ground by a defensive player who throws to a teammate who then tags the base before the runner reaches it. A *fly out* refers to a ball that is caught by a defensive player before it touches the ground.

How a Batter Reaches Base

If the batter avoids making an out, she can reach base in a variety of ways. One way is the base on balls. A batter is also awarded first base if she is hit by a pitch. Once the ball is hit, the batter can reach base with a single, double, triple, or home run—all called *base hits*. She can also reach base on an error by a defensive player, or by a *fielder's choice*, which means the defense chooses to get another base runner out while allowing the batter to reach base.

The Base Runner

Once a batter reaches base safely, she is considered to be a *base runner*. There are five basic rules that base runners must obey to avoid being called out. First, all base runners must occupy a base. Two players can never occupy the same base. Second, one base runner can never pass another on the base paths. Third, base runners cannot advance on a fly out until the ball has been caught

A runner is out if tagged before reaching the base.

(this is called *tagging up*). Fourth, the base runner cannot leave the base until the pitcher releases the ball; there is no leading off in softball. And fifth, when the ball is thrown back to the pitcher's circle, all base runners must go one way or another to reach a base, or they are out, unless the pitcher attempts to make a play on the base runner who is off a base.

Once a player is on base, a variety of things can happen.

A Sample Half Inning

There are countless possible scenarios that can take place in a given half inning, but there are plays and occurrences that are more common than others. The following section presents a sample half inning of play and includes a series of situations that your team is likely to encounter.

The first batter of the inning, after arriving at a comfortable stance in the batter's box, is ready to hit, and the umpire points at the pitcher as if to say, "Play ball!" The batter doesn't swing at the first pitch, but it's called a strike because it crossed the outside corner of the plate. The batter also lets the next pitch go by, but it's too high and is called a ball. On the third pitch, the batter swings and fouls the ball to the backstop, forcing the count to 1 and 2. The fourth pitch is out of the strike zone, but the batter swings and misses. Strike three is called, and the batter is out. One out, nobody on base, no runs scored.

The second batter is thrown two balls and, on the 2–0 count, hits a line-drive double down the right field line and into the corner. One out, runner on second base, no runs scored.

The third batter reaches a 0–1 count and then hits a ground ball that goes up the middle past the pitcher for a single. The runner who previously hit the double heads toward third base and is signaled by the third-base coach to try for home. The throw from the center fielder is thrown to the first-base player, who is acting as the cutoff person. There is no chance for the runner to be thrown out at home, so the catcher calls for the throw to be cut. This allows the first runner on base to score but keeps the runner who hit the ball from running to second base. One out, runner on first base, one run scored.

The fourth batter grounds a 3–1 pitch to the third-base player, who bobbles the ball and does not attempt a throw to first base. The batter reaches first base safely while the runner previously on first advances to second base. The play is ruled an error on the third-base player. One out, runners on first and second base, one run scored.

The fifth batter hits a fly ball to right field. The runner on first base positions herself halfway between first and second base so that if the ball is caught, she can return safely to first base, and if the ball is dropped, she can run to second base without being thrown out. The fly ball is caught by the right fielder, and the batter is out. As soon as the fly ball is caught by the right fielder, the runner on first base retreats to first while the runner on second tags up and runs to third base. The throw from right field is relayed by the second-base player to third base, but the throw is late and the runner is safe. Two outs, runners on first and third base, one run scored.

The sixth batter is thrown four balls and reaches first base on a walk. The runner previously on first base is then forced to go to second. Two outs, bases are loaded (runners on first, second, and third base), one run scored.

The seventh batter hits the first pitch to the shortstop, who tosses to the second-base player. The throw beats the runner coming from first and forces her into an out. Regardless of whether the runner on third base reaches home plate before the force-out is made, this runner doesn't score because the third out is a force-out. Final tally for the half inning: one run scored, two base hits, one error.

How a Base Runner Makes an Out

A base runner can be forced into an out by the defense tagging the base that the runner must reach before she actually reaches it. This is called a *force-out*. A defensive player who has the ball can tag a base runner who is not safely on a base. This is called a *tag out*.

How a Base Runner Advances around the Bases

A base runner can advance from base to base via a base hit, an error, a wild pitch, a *passed ball* (a pitch that gets by the catcher), by *tagging up*, by being forced (due to a fielder's choice, base on balls, or the batter being hit by a pitch), or by *stealing*. Stealing is when a base runner attempts to run to the next base just as the pitch leaves the pitcher's hand. A base runner can steal second or third base, but in youth leagues stealing home may or may not be an option. A base runner can leave the base only after the pitcher releases the ball to home plate.

Basics of Pitching

Pitchers throw from the *pitcher's plate* or *rubber*, which is a rubber rectangle fixed in the ground in the center of the diamond. They are required to have the front foot touching the rubber as they pitch.

As previously mentioned, the strike zone is dependent on the size of the batter and invokes the subjective judgment of the umpire. Pitchers need to be encouraged to maintain their composure and concentration on the mound. Whether an error is made by a teammate or the umpire makes a questionable call, pitchers need to respect the effort and judgment of both. As coach, you should never tolerate sour expressions or argumentative words from the pitcher to anyone else—umpires and other players included. They reflect poorly on the player, on you as coach, and on the player's parents, and it certainly makes throwing the next pitch for a strike even more difficult. As a fun learning activity, have each pitcher umpire during a scrimmage or a drill in practice sometime during the season. They'll all gain respect for just how hard it is to call balls and strikes.

Playing in the Spotlight

No other sports highlight and record every detail, every individual play, like softball and baseball. The individual parts in a softball game somehow become bigger than the whole picture, and for that reason, the individual player is cast into the spotlight. In a split second a player whose name hasn't been called all game is the one person who can make or break the game—and all eyes are fixed on her. Imagine your 10-year-old second-base player when she watches a ground ball go through her legs with the tying runner on third base, and picture her reaction. The spotlight is on her. She knows she goofed, and what she needs at that moment is encouragement and support, not criticism. Wait for the end of the inning, when your player is out of the spotlight, to tell her what caused her to commit that error.

The T-Ball Experience

T-ball is a gentle, nurturing introduction to softball or baseball. Played by 4- to 8-year-olds, the game is intentionally structured to expose kids to the basics without imposing too many rules. The T-ball veterans on your team will likely have a firmer grasp of fundamentals than your other players, but don't expect them to have *too* much of a lead on kids who haven't played at all.

In T-ball, the offensive team hits a ball off a waist-level batting tee. There's no intimidating pitcher, and players won't fear being hit by an errant pitch. This allows the ball to be put into play more easily, giving both offense and defense a chance to play.

Everyone plays in a T-ball game. There are no strikeouts, no walks, and the offensive team is retired only when all players have had a turn to bat, which leads to longer innings and sometimes astronomical scores. On defense every player takes the field. If you've ever watched kids in action during a T-ball game, you've noted that rules are much looser and total chaos is no stranger.

But that's just the point. Kids learn to catch, throw, run the bases, and hit the ball. And most important, kids have fun as they learn the game.

The Batter's Box

On each side of home plate is a 3- by 7-foot painted rectangle called the *batter's box*. The batter is required to stand within the box and should stand close enough to the plate so that, when she swings, the barrel of the bat can reach the outside part of the strike zone. Young players have a tendency to stand too far from the plate for fear of being hit by the pitch, so you need to encourage them to step up to the plate and be willing to swing aggressively.

The On-Deck Circle

The player waiting to hit next swings and warms up in the *on-deck circle*. This is often a dirt or painted circle located in foul territory and out of the way of the bench. All of the equipment should be kept in the bench or dugout area, away from batters warming up or coming into the dugout. The on-deck batter should always wear a helmet when warming up.

Responsibilities of a Coach during the Game

Game coaching is covered in much greater detail in chapter 7, but these are the basics. You are responsible for assigning positions and making sure that you have nine players in their appropriate positions for each inning.

You need to establish a substitution schedule for each game that allows equal playing time to all players who share positions (more on this in chapter 7). While your team is at bat, you are responsible for having first-base and third-base coaches in their respective coach's box located in foul territory beside the respective base. Though it is not required, I suggest that you be the third-base coach and either use your assistant as first-base coach or (if you don't have an assistant available) create a rotating schedule of players (with helmets on) who will be the first-base coach. This keeps the players who are not currently in the game still involved in the action. As third-base coach, you are responsible for calling specific plays and for directing the runners around the base paths.

Defensively you need to be constantly aware of your players' positioning, making sure that they are where they should be. Young infielders have a tendency to gravitate toward the bases while outfielders tend to migrate toward the foul lines. You need to keep an eye on them and make sure that they stay at their positions. You are also responsible for monitoring your pitcher's physical and mental condition on the field, and for making pitching changes if the need arises.

Basic Safety Measures

Softball is a game played with swinging bats, hard balls, and fixed objects like backstops and fences. Common sense goes a long way in forming a safe playing environment, but without taking necessary safety precautions, it can be a very dangerous game. If you are aware of the areas of potential danger and are diligent in creating and maintaining a safe environment, you can make it safe. Below is a list containing areas of concern and how to avoid injury.

Helmets

Most of us would not allow our children to get on a bicycle without wearing a helmet, and the same thing stands true for softball players on offense. Helmets must be worn by all players at bat and on the base paths. Coaches, players rotating through the hitting drills outlined in chapter 6, and players who are practicing their swings in the on-deck circle all should wear helmets as well. Any player who is on deck or preparing to swing a bat must check around her for other players, and team members need to be reminded to stay away from the on-deck circle if they are not warming up to bat. If a player is not in the game or in one of these "helmet situations," she must stay behind the fence. And perhaps most importantly, encourage your players to stay alert during the game. In a fun and positive manner, periodically quiz the players on the bench on the number of outs, the count of balls and strikes, what they would do if the ball were hit to them, and other points

---

The Discovery Method, Part 1

One of the most effective ways of teaching children a skill is to use the *discovery method*—where they discover the answer for themselves. Here's how it works: you give them a demonstration of the technique you want them to do. For example, if you wanted to teach them how to catch a ball properly, instead of saying "Trap the ball in the pocket of the glove," say "Watch this. You tell me where the ball goes when I hold up my glove." Let your players tell you what is going on with the drill, so they explain it to you.

Focus on Skill Components

Good softball is all about honing the basics of throwing, catching, hitting, and fielding through lots and lots of repetitions during practices. You can keep your players excited about practicing the same skills over and over by breaking a skill down into its components and working on each one in a slightly different way. For example, when we practice hitting, I often set up stations where players move from activity to activity, working on individual aspects of their swings at each station. Creating variations of the same thing is a great way for players to practice their skills in a fun and exciting manner.

about the game. This not only promotes safety, but it conditions the mental aspect of their development as players.

Communication

Defensive players chasing after fly balls tend to have their heads up while they run. As a result, players can collide with other players or objects such as fences. For this reason, it is crucial that you teach your players to communicate. Players who are not in pursuit of the ball should let those who are chasing it know where the fence is. And if two players are after the same fly ball, they need to communicate by calling "Mine, mine!" and the other player yells "Go!" Fly Balls in Two Lines gives players practice at calling for the ball (see drill D8 on page 100).

Throwing

At the beginning of each practice and game have your team assemble to warm up and throw, as in One-Knee Throwing, Close and One-Knee Throwing, Far (see drills W2 and W3 on pages 88, 89). Players should

For safety's sake, players on the bench should be taught to pay attention to the game at all times.

never walk behind other throwers, they should always throw in the same direction, parallel to one another, and partners should make eye contact with one another before making a throw. If a throw is missed, the player jogs after the ball and then jogs back to the throwing position. She should *not* throw from where she picks up the ball. When you yell, "Hold the ball!" players should stop throwing immediately and follow your next instruction.

Batting

Players must stay clear of players who may be swinging bats, and a player planning to swing must check all around her to make sure that no one is in jeopardy of being hit. It is possible that bats can be released in the follow-through of a swing, and for this reason, players should never stand behind a batter. This includes batters at the plate as well as those who are hitting off of batting tees, hitting in a Soft Toss drill (see drill B3 on pages 105–6), or simply taking practice swings without a ball. The Single and Double Tee Hits and Soft Toss drills (see drills B1, B2, and B3 on pages 104–6) also require a fence or a screen into which players hit balls. Make sure that the fence or screen has no pipes or cross-pieces that could cause the ball to carom and end up hitting a player. The players can hit into netting, out into the field, or into the fence with whiffle or softie balls. Softie balls are the same size as regular softballs, but are made of soft material. Do not hit softballs into chain-link fences. Finally, train your players to set the bat down after hitting the ball and before running to a base. Throwing the bat is a common problem among young players, and it puts both catchers and umpires in jeopardy.

Sliding

In softball, diving and bent-leg slides are common. Both slides are described in chapter 4 (see pages 50–51) and should be taught so that the player's head and face are always up and away from balls, gloves, and cleats. It is also important that players not slide into first base except to avoid a tag or a collision. It is safer and, in fact, faster to simply run through the base.

Throwing Arms

To reduce the potential of injury to their throwing arms, players should always warm up their arms slowly each day and gradually add time and dis-

Don't Encourage Strikes!

Fast-pitch pitching is very different from baseball pitching. In an average inning, a developing pitcher may hit several players and walk even more—it's really very common. The development of the pitcher in softball is entirely different than in baseball, and it's very important for a coach *not* to demand the pitcher throw strikes above all else. If the player is truly unable to throw with the proper mechanics, with more pitches over the plate than not, she is probably not ready to pitch in a game yet.

When Your Pitcher Is in Trouble

One way to help young pitchers is to predetermine the number of innings they'll pitch. You may have several players on your team who want to pitch, so decide beforehand how many innings each will be on the mound. Let them pitch those innings, regardless of how badly the inning may be going. Definitely explain to the entire team that learning to pitch is an important and often difficult part of the game, and that the team supports the pitcher 100 percent. On the other hand, if your pitcher starts to cry or break down or is noticeably upset, go to the mound, bring her out of the game, and reassure her immediately.

tance to build strength and stamina. Proper throwing mechanics are essential to preventing throwing injuries.

Fast-pitch pitching mechanics require two things that go together simultaneously: speed and proper mechanics. This means that a lot of the pitches don't go where they should. When developing pitchers try to throw strikes too early, they almost always try to bowl the ball to get it over the plate. This alters the important balance of developing speed and good mechanics first, and it can permanently damage a developing pitcher's long-term potential pitching ability. Encourage your player to do her best, but not necessarily to just "get it over the plate."

Setting Up the Season

Your duties as the coach of a youth softball team most likely won't end when you walk off the field; you'll also be the team administrator, equipment manager, and CEO. But just because you're in charge doesn't mean you'll have to go it alone. The best way to get your season running smoothly, enabling you to focus your energy on coaching your players, is to be well prepared.

Create the Practice and Game Schedule

Before a single ball is batted or catch is made, you should have a schedule of practices and games for the entire season. Depending on the age of your players and the access you'll have to playing fields, I recommend two to three practices a week for older (10 and up) players and one to two practices a week for players under 10. Try to keep practices and games on the same days of the week and same time of day throughout the season—it is much easier for families to commit to a consistent schedule than one that varies widely. Once your season starts, you may find you won't have the need—or the time—for any practices if your team plays two or more games

A Word on Tryouts

As a coach of a team of 8- to 12-year-olds, you're unlikely to face the prospects of formal tryouts, those often nerve-wracking sessions in which a group of coaches evaluates potential players on such skills as throwing, catching, baserunning, hitting, and fielding. As kids work their way into more competitive leagues when they're older, tryouts are necessary. But not now.

Tryouts have no place in a youth league at this level. Your league might bring kids together before the season to allow coaches to distribute experienced players evenly, but this session should be no more than that. Your first priority is to teach softball fundamentals and allow the kids to enjoy themselves. Your players might be fresh from T-ball, or they might have no experience at all. The drills and advice in this book are designed to allow you to work with everyone, regardless of skill and experience.

Key to Success: Put That in Writing

Here are some issues you may want to address in your letter to parents:

- Your coaching philosophy, including your attitude toward winning and losing, teamwork, and your over-all objective of developing skills and having fun.

- Expectations for sportsmanship and behavior at practice and games—for players, parents, and you.

- Goals for the season: what you want your players to get out of it, and what you want to get out of it.

- Policies for tardiness, absence from games or practices, discipline issues.

a week. If your players have games only once a week or once every two weeks, you may want to hold practices to work on things that have come up in the games. Have this schedule of practices and games ready to hand out at the first practice so that every parent has a copy and knows what kind of commitment they are making to the team.

Meet with Parents

It's very important that you either meet in person with parents or send a letter home to them that outlines your philosophy of the game and the expectations you have for sportsmanship and participation during the season (see the sample letter on page 24). Parents and players will need to both hear and see what you expect from them in terms of good sportsmanship, competition, being on time, participation in games, and so on. Establishing the ground rules before the season begins means that everyone is fully aware of what you expect from them, yourself, and the team for the season.

During the team meeting, solicit feedback and suggestions from parents about their expectations for the season, concerns about their children, and how they would like to participate. Now is the time to recruit parent volunteers to help with phone trees (see page 25 for a more detailed explanation of phone trees), carpooling, fund-raising, and the many other administrative tasks that come with being part of a league. You'll find that most parents are happy and eager to help. Give them as many responsibilities as possible for *off*-field jobs, so that you can concentrate on coaching.

If you find that a face-to-face meeting with all parents is impossible to schedule, make sure you call each player's parent or guardian to introduce yourself. Briefly communicate your philosophy of coaching and your expectations, ask whether there is anything you should know concerning their child, and allow them time to respond and ask questions. This gives parents an opportunity to discuss any concerns or issues they may have in a private setting. Also during this phone call be sure to remind them of the date and time of the first practice.

Sample Preseason Letter to Parents

Dear Parents:

Another softball season is upon us. I'm excited about our team and hope your kids are, too.

My primary goal for the season is for everyone to have fun and improve their softball skills. My basic philosophy is to foster a positive, supportive atmosphere so that every player has a great experience. Regardless of ability, every member of the team deserves to be treated with encouragement. Players should respect each other on and off the field and should learn both to win and to lose well. I look to you to help reinforce these important concepts. When you come to games or practices, please limit your interaction with your children to positive encouragement from a distance. During games, please treat the umpires with the respect they deserve. We are our children's most important role models. I'll set as good an example as I possibly can, and I would greatly appreciate your help by doing the same.

Games: Please make every effort to arrive at games 30 minutes before the scheduled start. If you know that getting your child to a game will be difficult, we can carpool. If your child can't make it to a game, please let me know in advance. If she misses practice the week before the game without a good reason, she might not play in the game. Please know that I have this policy so that participation in the games is fair for everyone.

Cancellation: Unless you hear otherwise, we'll always have practice or games. In the case of cancellation, kids will be notified either at school or by means of the enclosed phone tree.

Must Bring: Please make sure that your child has a water bottle, glove, and sneakers or rubber cleats. These, and other personal equipment, should be labeled with her name.

We're looking forward to a great season of softball. If you have questions or concerns, please feel free to contact me.

Thanks,
The Coach
250 Main Street
555-3303
coach@softball.com

Finding an Assistant

You will find that it is crucial to have some help out on the field during practice. Ideally you should have one or two people who can commit a good chunk of time to being your assistant, but if you need to schedule a rotating list of volunteers for each practice, it is still better than trying to go it alone.

You may be able to find a local high school or university student to assist you. He or she might have better rapport with the players, and may be able to demonstrate skills you can't. But your largest pool will be parents.

Make sure that each assistant shares your philosophy of coaching *and* your methods. Meet with your assistants before the first practice to go over the list of skills you want to work on, the methods you'll use to teach them, and why you use these methods. Remember that your philosophy is the philosophy that your team will live by, and your assistants

An assistant coach can be a great help to you. If she's an older player, she'll serve as a good role model for your players.

Calling All Volunteers!

Here are some ways that supportive parents and friends can help you and the team make the season run smoothly.

Phone Tree

It is important to have a good communication system so that 18 softball players or parents aren't calling you every time it rains. One of the most important jobs a helpful parent can do is set up a phone-tree calling protocol for bad weather, cancelled games, etc. The way the phone tree works is that you call the designated parent with whatever message you want to convey, and that parent relays the message to the rest of the team through a chain of communication.

Travel Plans

When your team has an away game, it is a good idea to have a central meeting place to start the trip so that everyone gets off at the same time. A parent volunteer can be responsible for arranging carpooling, distributing maps or instructions for getting to the field, etc.

Uniforms and Equipment

Many youth league players come to their first few practices without the proper equipment. One way to avoid this is to have a parent volunteer arrange a sign-up night at the local sports store so that the kids are signed up for the team and outfitted at the same time. Most sports stores will give significant discounts for team purchases. If you have extra gloves or your league has extra equipment available, try to bring it to practice for kids who don't have their own.

Team Dinners, Fund-Raisers, and All That Other Stuff

Most youth league teams need to raise money for one thing or another, and any team worth its stuff will have at least one team dinner during the season. These events are great for fostering team spirit. A parent volunteer can be in charge of these events and can take advantage of the talents and expertise of the other parents on the team as well.

Set the Ground Rules with Your Assistant

Make sure that you explain your philosophy and expectations for behavior during the season, not only to your players and their parents but to your assistants as well. You don't want to be out on the field with an assistant who doesn't share your philosophy of good sportsmanship, patience, or keeping things fun, and you need to make this clear before the season starts.

need to respect and reinforce this to your players. The last thing you'll want is to have two different coaches telling your players two entirely different ways of doing things.

Appropriate Numbers of Players on the Team

The ideal number of players on a softball team is 15, but if you have as few as 13 or as many as 18, you can still manage. It's unlikely that you'll have the exact number you want. Fewer than 13 players can make it difficult to fill out the field if more than a few people are absent or injured, but it is also an opportunity for players to try a variety of positions. Larger numbers of players usually mean that playing time is shortened for everyone and there is less individual attention. However, the important point, regardless of the number of players you have, is that everyone has an opportunity to play and learn.

Equipment

Softball is a fairly equipment-intensive sport. It's important to take an inventory of the equipment your league has already and to determine what you'll need to get. Whatever your rec league can't provide, you can acquire through fund-raising events, parental donations, or a personal investment (equipment bought in bulk is considerably less expensive). Each player should be responsible for her own glove, knee pads, batting glove, water bottle, and softball shoes. You can decide if you want your players to bring their own bats, helmets, and other personal equipment to practices and games. If so, be sure to make it a policy that all personal equipment is well labeled and the responsibility of the owner, not the coach.

Some leagues supply their players with uniforms, which usually consist of a T-shirt,

Be as organized with your equipment as you are with your players.

Separate Teaching from the Game

As a general rule it is better to save your teaching for practice, rather than trying to combine playing in a competitive game with teaching new skills. Keep the teaching points to a minimum during games and allow your players to focus on the task at hand. However, if you have a large team with many nonstarters on the bench, using game examples as teaching points can be productive.

Equipment Checklist

- Aluminum bats
- Softballs
- Helmets
- Catcher's gear
- Equipment bags (bat bag, helmet bag, ball bag, catcher's gear bag)
- Protective screens (available at sporting goods stores)
- First-aid kit with ointment and ice packs
- Clipboard, scorebook
- Team roster

shorts or pants, and a hat or visor. If your league does not provide these, you or a delegated parent should make arrangements with a local sporting goods store to order them *before the season starts*. Sizing, especially for catcher's gear, is very important. Ask for tips on proper fit at your local sports store or from other coaches.

At a minimum, your team will need the following equipment:

- 8 batting helmets of various sizes
- 5–6 bats that are sized to the age group you are coaching
- catcher's gear (catcher's mitt, chest protector, shin pads, a helmet, and face mask with helmet piece)
- 1–2 protective screens
- various softballs: real softballs (11-inch size for younger players up to 13 years), "softie" or training balls
- batting tees
- throw-down plates for batting practice
- if possible, a pitching machine

If your town or city has a college or university fast-pitch softball team, don't hesitate to contact the coach or go to one of their practices. See what equipment and devices they use that might work well for you and ask for advice.

For games, you'll need a scorebook, equipment bags, and a first-aid kit that must include ointment for abrasions and ice packs.

Keeping Your Eye on the Ball (and Bats, and Everything Else)

To lighten your load, assign different players the job of carrying each equipment bag from your car to the field and back again after practice. Each week, change the rotation of jobs and instill in your players a sense of pride for doing their respective jobs well.

Questions and Answers

Q. No parents have volunteered to help with the administrative tasks, and I'm feeling completely overwhelmed. What do I do?

A. Don't feel shy about calling parents and asking them to get involved

The Tools of Ignorance

Anyone who has ever had the unique opportunity to crouch behind home plate for seven innings trying to catch or block every pitch that is thrown is struck at some point with two realizations. The first one is, "Boy am I glad I'm wearing all of this gear." And the second develops into something like this: "There must be an easier way to play this game!"

Catchers are the kids on your team who love to get dirty and want to be a constant part of the action. The equipment today is very well made and does a great job of protecting young catchers. So before these prospects know any better, take advantage of their ignorance and dress them in "the tools." The position is made for them. Look for youngsters who are physically tough and natural leaders.

in the administrative details. Just because no one has volunteered doesn't mean parents wouldn't be willing to help with one or more specific projects if you ask them. Take charge and stress to them that the more they help, the better their child's season will be. Usually people like to help; they are just waiting to be asked.

Q. Most of the parents I've talked to don't have time to have a "parents-only" meeting with me. Do I call each one individually, write a letter, or what? How important is it to meet with them before the season?

A. Meet with those who can come to discuss the season. For those who can't make it, write up your expectations and rules, and put out a letter to them. (Actually, it's a good idea to send that letter to all the parents.) If they disagree with what you've written, they can get in touch with you to talk about it. It's a good idea to give parents a choice of meeting with you, regardless of how many can come, to keep the lines of communication open.

Q. One of my players cannot afford to buy a glove. How should I deal with this?

A. Every player needs a glove, plain and simple. Ask around discreetly if your friends or acquaintances have an extra glove they can lend the team. Similarly, go to a sporting goods store with which you have already established a relationship and see if they'd be willing to donate a glove to the team for the season. Also check with your league. They may have funds set up for situations like these. Local public school athletic directors may also be able to help.

Q. Where do I find out the details of practice and game scheduling? Do I have to call coaches to set up games? Is this something I have to take care of myself, or does the league do it, or what?

A. It depends on whether your town or school sponsors the league. If the school sets it up, contact the athletic director or physical education

Matching Bat to Batter

Most young players between the ages of 8 and 12 should not use a bat larger than a 28-inch, 22-ounce bat. But size depends on a player's height and strength. If you're not sure what size bats you have or if the bat is appropriate for the batter, watch your players swing. If they swing the bat and it dips as it goes around, the bat is too heavy. If the bat is level through the swing, it is probably the proper weight.

It's important that your players have bats they can handle. Make sure you have equipment sized for younger players.

teacher. If the town sponsors the league, talk to the director of the recreation department. You might find that everything is done for you, from field time to game scheduling. It is useful to have the names and phone numbers of the other coaches in case, for example, there is ever a question of game cancellation.

There are rules and details specific to each league that every new coach needs to learn, so if your recreation department or school holds any league meetings, make every effort to attend. Not only is the information discussed in these meetings helpful, but the interaction with veteran coaches who attend is invaluable.

Q. I'm having trouble drafting my letter to parents about what I expect from the season. I don't want to offend anyone, or hurt anyone's feelings.

A. Remember two things: one, this does not have to be the Gettysburg Address, and two, you are the leader of the team and the one responsible for setting its tone, goals, and rules. Simple is definitely better—the fewer rules you have, the fewer opportunities for you to be backed into a corner, with a parent or player stating, "But your letter said . . ." In a short letter, let the parents know how excited you are to be coaching, articulate your main goals of fun and development, and continually stress the positive. Be upbeat, say what you mean and mean what you say, and be confident in your convictions. Feel free to use our sample letter, either word for word or just to get you started. And be sure to have someone proofread your letter before you send it out.

CHAPTER 4

Essential Skills—and How to Teach Them

Anyone who watched the U.S. women's national softball team in the 2000 Olympics was impressed with the effortless way they made spectacular catches, fired blazing pitches past batters, and hit the ball right up the middle of the field. But underneath all of that flash and skill is the time spent working on the basic fundamentals of the game. Even the world's best softball players practice the basics every single day, and your job as coach is to help your players understand and practice the fundamentals to give them a solid skills foundation.

Catching

I have always stressed to my players that the team that "plays catch" well is the team that will be most successful in games. Throwing and catching the ball are perhaps the most important skills a ballplayer needs to learn to play the game, and good catching and good throwing go together.

The Principles

It is important for players to learn to receive the ball in such a way that they can then make the best throw possible. The keys to catching include setting up to receive the ball, using two hands, and preparing to throw.

Setting up to receive the catch

When the ball has been hit or thrown, the fielder should move to position herself to catch the ball on the throwing side of her body. A common mistake young players make is to move their gloves, not their bodies, to the ball. The player should try to catch the ball at chest height toward the middle of her body, so that she can make the transition to throwing quickly and efficiently.

Using two hands

When the ball comes into her glove, the player should immediately secure the catch with her throwing hand by covering the ball in the pocket of her glove.

Preparing to throw

As the player receives the ball, she turns sideways to her throwing target by setting her back foot perpendicular to the target and pointing her front foot toward her target. Putting her feet in these positions helps to ensure that the player doesn't throw the ball from an open position. Rather, she uses the strength of her torso for throwing momentum.

Running catches

Balls can't always be caught when the player is in a stationary position. Running catches, or catches made to the far glove-hand side or far throwing-hand side of the body require specific glove-work. Neither of these particular types of catches can be made using two hands. A catch made to the far glove-hand side—called a *forehand*—is made with the fingers below and the thumb on top. When making a forehand catch, a player reaches to the ball with the glove-hand-side leg. A *backhand* catch is made to the far throwing-hand side of the body with the fingers above and the thumb below. To make this play, a player crosses her glove-hand-side leg over the other leg and reaches toward the ball.

Two-handed catches: Whether catching a ground ball (left) or a fly ball (right) always secure the ball in the glove with your throwing hand.

Softballs are tough to hold, especially for small hands. Grip the ball with the fingertips—don't palm it.

Throwing

The Principles

Throwing is a fluid motion made up of very specific components that need to work together seamlessly. The key parts to a throw are the proper grip on the ball, arm action, and footwork.

Grip

One of the keys to a proper throw is gripping the ball with the fingertips of the hand, not the palm. Players should grip the ball along its four horizontal seams. To help your players remember which direction the seams of the softball should face in their hands, tell them to look for the "C" in the ball and use it as a guide.

The middle finger of the throwing hand should be on one seam, with the thumb on the opposite side of the ball. The pointer and ring finger should be on the other seam. Placing the fingertips on the ball seams helps provide a much more reliable grip on the ball. Players should not palm the ball; rather, there should be a space between the ball and the palm of the hand.

Because some younger players may have trouble gripping standard-size softballs, youth leagues may also accept 11-inch balls.

Arm Action

When players throw a softball, it is very important for them to throw, not push, the ball to its target. They should not "wrap" their hand around the ball (also known as palming the ball), but maintain a loose but firm grip on

Learning to Throw Effectively

Virtually all young children begin throwing balls by pushing the ball away from their bodies rather than using hip and body rotation to generate power, primarily because their abdominal and hip flexor muscles lack strength. As they get older and stronger, children become better throwers through trial and error and years of softball practice—they achieve harder, faster, and farther throws through proper trunk rotation. Children who don't play softball early or long enough to learn proper arm action or how to close up their bodies and use the power generated from good hip and torso rotation to power their throws often rely on pushing the ball from an open position that they used as a young child. But even children with relatively less muscle mass can learn to throw with sound mechanics if they are taught proper footwork, trunk rotation, and arm action at an early age. Their throwing muscles may not be as strong, and thus not as explosive as those of throwers with longer experience and more developed muscles, but they can learn proper throwing mechanics and become very accurate and efficient throwers.

it. The key to this is for the player to keep her hand behind the ball at all times during the throw. She should bring the ball back so there is a 90-degree angle from her hand to her armpit and elbow. The ball should face in the opposite direction, so if the player looks back over her shoulder, she will see the back of her hand, *not* the ball. Leading with her elbow, the player brings her arm around with her hand behind the ball at all times. When releasing the ball, the throwing arm should follow through to the opposite side of the body with the hand coming down below her waist. The player should try to spin or rotate the ball out of her hand, releasing it with a snap of the wrist.

Foot Action and Transition

The player's back foot should always be perpendicular to her target, her front foot pointing to the target at a 45-degree angle and her body sideways to the target. The transition from receiving the ball to throwing the ball is crucial; the more correct the feet are, the more accurate the throw. Because outfielders and infielders make different-length throws, each position has its own length of arm swing when making the transition from catching to throwing.

The outfield crow-hop: Outfielders use their whole bodies to throw, and the crow-hop helps an outfielder to gather crucial momentum while properly setting her feet to throw. A right-handed thrower, after making a catch, steps forward onto her left foot and hops forward, turning her body sideways to the target, crossing her right leg over and in front of the left.

When the right foot lands, it should be perpendicular to the target. Once in this position, the mechanics are identical to the basic throwing motion described above. A left-handed thrower simply uses the opposite footwork. As the crow-hop is taking place, the player should be transferring the ball from her glove to her throwing hand. The Three-Player Throwing drill (see drill D2 on pages 98–99) is good practice for this skill.

The infield "replace your feet": This technique allows infielders to quickly build necessary momentum toward first base, or whatever target to which they might be throwing.

Good throwing form calls for the player's back foot to be perpendicular to her target, her front foot pointing to the target at a 45-degree angle and her body sideways to the target.

This technique is identical to the outfield crow-hop *except* that the player's feet are closer together, and the movement should be as quick as possible.

Infield Defense

Fielding a ground ball is much harder than it looks. Even the smoothest, best-groomed field has irregularities, and when a spinning, bouncing ball makes contact, there's no guarantee where it will go. Practicing the proper fundamentals will help players avoid costly infield errors.

The Principles

The fundamentals of fielding a ground ball include three components: preparation, good body positioning, and proper hand positioning.

Infielder ready: feet spread, knees flexed, glove down and ready for anything.

Preparation

The infielder stands with her feet slightly beyond shoulder-width apart, knees flexed, weight on the balls of her feet, head up, and glove hand open.

This *athletic stance* allows the player to make quick and aggressive movement toward the ball when it is hit so that she can field the easiest bounce. Girls sometimes let their feet "duck out." Encourage them to keep their toes straight or slightly "toed in." In this stance the player's hands and glove are together and in front of her body, and her eyes are on the batter.

Different playing positions require different ready stances and hand positioning for the best fielding. Players at first and third base should be as low as possible in the athletic stance, with their gloves out, open to the batter, and close to the ground. Players at shortstop and on second base should have their hands and arms hanging down at knee height and open toward the batter ready for action. Outfielders should stand relaxed and upright, facing square to the batter (not turned to one side or the other), with hands and glove at waist height.

The Athletic Stance

Sports should be played in the *athletic stance* — the optimal body position for quickness and balance. A player in the athletic position has her weight slightly forward on the balls of the feet. The feet are just wider than shoulder width apart, and the knees are flexed. The upper body is straight, eyes are up, and the arms and hands are relaxed and ready for action. Impress upon your players that they play in games the way they practice. As a result, encourage them to practice in the athletic stance, and they'll see improvement in their play.

Hand positioning

It is very important to instill in your players the idea that fielding should be done with two hands whenever possible. The glove should be flat on the ground so that the back of the hand is on the ground, with the fingertips facing up slightly. When fielding a ball, the throwing hand should cover the ball as soon as the ball enters the glove.

The infielder moves to her left for a forehand grab of a ground ball (left). A backhand catch (right) requires more skill and timing.

The fielder should then bring the glove into her body and get a good grip on the ball. Most errors occur when players try to make the transition from fielding to throwing too quickly, before getting a good grip on the ball.

Sometimes fielding the ball with two hands in the middle of the body isn't an option. Ground balls hit to the far right or left of the body require forehands and backhands, which are plays made only with an outstretched glove. Any time a player is making such a play, she should keep her glove as close to the ground as possible; it is much easier to bring the glove up to adjust for an upward hop than to adjust down to a ball that may slide under her glove. Similar to catching a ball on either the left or right side of her body, a player making a forehand play on the ground should extend her leg on the glove-hand side of her body toward the ball. The webbing and fingers of her glove will be palm up when fielding a forehand ground ball. When fielding a backhand ground ball, the webbing and fingers of the glove will be down as the player extends her glove in front of her body. Backhands are one of the most difficult infield plays, since keeping the glove open is very challenging.

Conquering Fear of the Ball: Fielders

All young players, and many older players, have a real fear of being hit by batted balls, particularly hard ground balls. The first thing players need to learn is how to catch a thrown ball properly—a ball that is thrown low, high, to the glove side, to the throwing-hand side, and directly at them.

Teaching your players good fielding position and how to approach a ground ball will also go a long way toward alleviating both the fear of being hit and their chances of being caught unprepared. Roll ground balls until the players gain confidence in their fielding techniques. The more the fielders get their hands out in front and stay low, the better they can track the ball into the glove and protect themselves. Then hit short (40-foot) easy fungoes, or soft, practice fly balls. Rolled ground balls and short fungoes should be a part of every practice.

X Marks the Spot in the Infield

A good way to demonstrate where the ball should be fielded, and to help teach fielders to reach out for the ball, is to have each fielder bend over, reach out to the ground in front of her as far as she comfortably can without falling over, and mark an "X" in the dirt. This is the location where she should field the ball. Most players try to field the ball too close to their bodies and too far back in their stance. By marking the ground with an X, the player will have a visual reminder to field the ball at the proper distance from her body.

Ready for the tag. The infielder blocks one half of the base and has a firm grip on the ball (left). The infielder is in great position to tag the sliding runner (right).

Tag outs and put outs

Infielders have two jobs: to field the ball and to tag runners who come into the base. When the play is a force-out, infielders should go to the bag and straddle it, while staying on the infield side of it, facing the direction from which the ball is coming. When the player who is throwing releases the ball, the fielder should put her strong foot on the bag and stretch to receive the throw. A right-handed player should place her right foot on the base, a left-handed player her left foot. Sometimes younger players have a hard time finding the base with their feet while waiting to receive the throw for the force-out. Encourage them to put a foot on the base first, wait for the ball to be released, and then stretch to receive the throw. Remind them that their feet aren't attached to the base; it is more important to catch the ball than to keep their feet in place. Bad throws are common, and they should always leave the bag to get to the ball first and then go tag the base.

Bobbling Ball? Stop and Drop

If a player has bobbled the ball while fielding and can't make a clean catch, the best way to regain control is to stop and let the ball drop to the ground. Then she can pick it up with two hands, get a good grip on the ball, and usually still make the play. It takes much less time to stop and regroup than to frantically juggle a miscaught ball, and the out can usually still be made.

For a tag out, the fielder should square up to the source of the throw. She should straddle the bag as described above, while trying to "take away" half of the bag from the runner by staying on the infield part of the bag and forcing the runner to use the outside of the bag. When making a tag, the player should sweep the tag with a backhand technique. This will help protect the ball from being knocked out of her glove as it comes in contact with the runner.

Infielders should also learn and practice the *flip*, which is a short, underhanded toss used at short range, most often between the shortstop and second-base player when making force-outs and double plays. The player making the flip takes a long step toward her target with her glove-side foot and holds the ball with her fingers underneath and next to the hip. She keeps her glove to her chest so the base player can see the ball clearly and then tosses the ball to the base player without breaking her wrist so that the toss is a quick flip. When releasing the flip, she shouldn't let her throwing hand come above her shoulder; this assures a low toss.

On a force-out the infielder stretches to the throw, keeping contact with the base.

Outfield Defense

Outfielders have demanding, high-profile jobs—a fly ball is hit out of the infield, the runners are in scoring position, and all eyes are on the player under the ball. Will she catch it or won't she? It's all in the fundamentals.

The Principles

The keys for playing outfield defense involve good depth perception, good body position for catching a fly ball, and using two hands.

Fly balls

One of the most important aspects of catching a fly ball is being prepared to receive it. Ideally, the outfielder should always be in a position where she is catching the ball on the throwing side of her body, so she is immediately in position to make a good throw. Although this won't always happen, especially with young or inexperienced players, stress to players that they should always be behind the ball when catching it—it is always easier to run up to catch a ball that falls short than to try to react to a ball going over your head. Teach your outfielders to automatically take a step or two backward when the bat connects with the ball. Once the ball is in the air they can assess whether they need to run forward.

Once the outfielder has determined where she thinks the ball will land, she should run there as quickly as possible, set her feet with the throwing-side foot slightly in front of her glove-side foot, and prepare to receive the ball. The Quarterback Drill (see drill W9 on page 91) is excellent for teaching players to catch fly balls or any ball hit over any fielder's head.

Outfielder ready: knees flexed, feet spread, glove at waist level.

Using two hands

Outfielders should always try to catch fly balls between their chests and their eyes, *not* above or over their heads. This way they can see the ball at all times. The player should always try to catch the ball with two hands. As soon as the ball hits the glove pocket, the other hand should close over it to keep the ball inside.

Obviously not every fly ball will come directly where the outfielder has planted herself; some will require one-handed catches and running dives, but these kinds of plays can't be made with any kind of consistency until your players learn the basic fundamentals of catching fly balls properly.

Communication in the outfield

It is very important for outfielders to communicate with each other. When a fly ball is hit and three different players are running toward the ball with their heads pointed to the sky, collisions can happen. Teach your fielders to "call for the ball": this means that whichever outfielder is confident that she can catch the ball should call, "Mine, mine!" The other fielders should signal that they acknowledge her claim and call "Go!" This completes the communication and ensures that someone has taken responsibility for catching the ball. Generally speaking, the center fielder is the voice of authority in the outfield, so if she calls for the ball, the other fielders should back up the play. As soon as a player is confident she can catch the ball, she should call for it.

The other reason for communication between outfielders is to alert each other to obstacles on the field. The outfielders backing up the fielder making the play should keep aware of and inform the catching fielder of potential hazards, such as how far away the back fence is and how much space she has to make the catch. The other player can say "Room" to indicate the player has plenty of room to make the catch. This is for more advanced players.

Fielding ground balls in the outfield

Fielding ground balls in the outfield is based on the same principles as fielding grounders in the infield, but outfielders usually have the benefit of

Fly-Ball Priority

My recommendations for fly-ball priority are simple: outfielders have precedence over infielders, and center fielders have precedence over left or right fielders.

added time. Unless the outfielder is trying to throw someone out at a base, her primary job is to stop the ball in front of her and get it back to the infield to keep the runner from advancing. There are three techniques for fielding ground balls in the outfield, based on the action on the diamond.

Down-and-block technique

The *down-and-block technique*, as its name implies, is used when the outfielder wants to keep the ball in front of her by blocking it with her glove or body. It's usually used when there is no one on base. The fielder puts her glove-side knee to the ground, blocks the ball with her glove, squares her body to the ball, and throws it back to the infield. As long as the ball stays in front of the player, she doesn't necessarily need to field it cleanly.

Like an infielder

When runners are on base and a ground ball is hit to the outfield, the outfielder uses the same technique that is used in fielding a ball in the infield — she should keep the ball in front of her, reach down and out with a good athletic stance, and with two hands catch the ball, square up, and throw.

Fielding the ball this way puts the outfielder in a better position to throw if the runner tries to take an extra base.

Outfielders have the luxury of more time when fielding ground balls. That's more time to get in front of the ball and use the down-and-block technique.

On the charge

This is a risky but quick fielding technique that advanced players should attempt only if the game-winning run is at stake. The outfielder charges the ball, keeps her head down, and reaches down for the ball with one hand. She stays low, flexes her knees, and bends at the waist, getting the ball at her front foot, coming up, and throwing in one fluid motion. If the player misses on the charge, the ball will roll past her farther into the outfield. For this reason, a player should try it only in a "do or die" situation or if she is playing right field and attempts to field the ball on one bounce and throw out the runner at first base. This is an advanced technique.

Team Defense

The fundamental principle of team defense is to get the out on every play, which can eliminate a "big inning." This means making the safest plays, avoiding unnecessary throws, and communicating with your players. Each time a batter comes up, alert the team as to how many outs there are and where the easiest play will be. When your players are more confident with their skills and their roles on the field, assign someone the job of field leader, who can then alert her teammates to the plays. The leader is often the catcher, since she can see the entire field, but other players can be the leader as well.

Playing Catcher

The catcher is a crucial part of any softball team. Playing catcher can be a difficult job, and although your catcher should be one of the better players on your team, it is more important that whoever plays catcher *wants* to be playing catcher. Contrary to stereotype, the catcher doesn't need to be the biggest or strongest player on the team; rather, she needs to have quick hands, quick feet, and a great attitude. Although a strong arm is an asset, it is even better to have a player with a quick arm—a ball thrown from the catcher to second base that bounces and gets there quickly is better than a slow, high-arcing throw that gets there without a bounce.

The Principles

The catcher should make herself as small as possible behind the plate while at the same time providing a large strike target for her pitcher. The catcher should squat approximately three feet behind home plate with her weight evenly distributed, her glove arm stretched but not stiff-armed in front of her and her body always remaining square to the pitch because all of her equipment is designed to protect the front of her body.

Conquering Fear of the Ball: Catchers

Catchers need to be taught specific receiving techniques and drills, first in an upright (standing) position and then from a crouch.

Step 1: Use softie balls and have your catcher dress in full gear. Teach her proper glove action and footwork for pitches to various locations, including in the dirt and blocking techniques. Remind her also to protect her throwing hand.

Step 2: Once she's comfortable behind the plate, put a batter in the batter's box but tell her not to swing; instead, the batter should let the pitches go by so that the catcher learns how to focus on the pitch and not be distracted by the batter's presence.

Step 3: Have the batter swing through the pitches but intentionally miss so that the catcher learns to visually track the pitch to the mitt without flinching, turning her head, or blinking her eyes. First use a softie ball and then switch to a regular softball.

Step 4: Have the catcher catch live batting practice.

The catcher should develop the habit of keeping her throwing hand tucked behind her back so the fingers on her throwing hand aren't exposed. As she sets up to receive the ball, the catcher should make sure her elbow is outside of her knees. When the ball comes into her glove, she brings the ball and her throwing hand together up toward her right ear (if right-handed), simultaneously standing up and setting her feet to throw.

Throwing to the bases from home plate

The key to throwing to the bases from the catching position is quick feet. After the catcher has received the pitch, she brings the ball directly up to her ear on the throwing arm side, quickly jumps to her feet, stands sideways to her target, and throws the ball.

Blocking pitches

If a pitch goes into the dirt in front of the catcher, she should immediately bring her knees down to where her feet were and put her glove in the space on the ground between her knees. This will stop the pitch on the ground. The goal is to block the ball to keep it in front of her, not necessarily to catch it. Her shoulders should be curled, with her chin to her chest, and rounded so she can use her entire body to block the ball's motion. The fingers on her hand without the glove should be pointing down.

The catcher should be prepared for anything, such as a low ball. To catch a low ball, she drops down and uses her knees and glove to block the pitch.

Pitching

Although there are several different pitching deliveries, a windmill motion is most common. The pitcher starts with her front foot half on the rubber and her back toe touching the rubber. She separates her hands so the ball hand is not touching the glove hand. The right-handed player steps forward with her left leg, turning her body and opening it up sideways so both her back foot and her front foot are at a 45-degree angle to the catcher. Her right pitching arm makes one revolution with the arm straight but not locked, brushes her ear, and releases the ball at her hip area. The pitcher's torso should be straight up and down at the end of the pitch, not leaning forward with the follow through.

Pitchers should hold the ball the same way they hold it for overhand throwing: holding four seams, they should let the ball roll off the fingertips, rather than the palm of the hand. In pitching, the thumb is the first digit to let go of the ball in order to get the maximum spin possible.

Pitchers should throw the ball as hard as they can with the proper mechanics. Mechanics and speed go together simultaneously. Control comes later. When working with young and developing pitchers, it is important to do as many drills pitching to a target—whether it is throwing into a

The windmill pitch. Starting with both feet on the rubber, the pitcher steps forward with her left leg, turning her body and opening it up sideways. Her right arm makes one revolution with the arm straight but not locked, brushes her ear, and releases the ball at her hip area.

wall or into a net—as possible. If you have a player acting as a catcher, make sure that she is in full catching gear so the pitcher doesn't need to worry about hitting the catcher. It is also a good idea to put a bucket of balls next to the pitcher on the rubber so she doesn't have to waste time chasing balls. It is very common for beginning pitchers to stand 15–20 feet from a target such as a wall and only hit the wall occasionally—her pitches will be that wild. Over time she will gain control. It is vital never to sacrifice speed or mechanics for control when a pitcher is developing.

The Principles

When teaching pitching to young players it is best to break down the entire motion into its individual components. Start with the same drill progres-

How to Spot a Potential Pitcher

If you are trying to determine who on your team would make a good pitcher, look to the players with heart, determination, and the desire to pitch. While size can be a factor as players get older—tall players with longer arms have longer "levers" for throwing, and players with bigger hands can grip the ball with their fingertips—young players who show an interest in pitching should certainly be given an opportunity.

A good way to assess potential pitchers is to watch your players play catch throwing overhand. The player with the strongest overhand throw will likely be the kid who can throw it best underhand; the biomechanics of the fast-pitch pitching motion are very similar to, although the reverse of, the overhand throw.

Control Comes Last

There are three components to pitching: mechanics, speed, and control. You should teach speed and mechanics first, and simultaneously. Control will be the last thing pitchers will master, and it's important not to push them to throw strikes. Kids who throw for control first don't throw it very hard and usually don't succeed later on when speed becomes important. If you think some of your players have potential for future competitive play, be careful to stress mechanics and speed more than anything.

Everyone, especially parents and other players, needs to understand that no great pitcher has evolved without having those games where she walked eleven players and hit nine. It's part of the sport; pitching underhand is very difficult, and not as familiar as throwing overhand. Softball pitchers need to work separately and more often than any other position if they want to become really skilled—repetition pays off.

sion: wrist snap, one-knee arm circles, half strides, and finally, full pitches. Players learning to pitch can pitch to a wall or fence with a softie ball, and should not pitch to another player. Nonhuman targets are important so the kids continue to throw the ball hard as they are learning control.

Wrist snap

A key element of effective pitching is how fast the player can throw the ball and how much wrist snap she can give it. The pitcher keeps her hand behind the ball and snaps it through, releasing the ball. The arm then comes up and bends at the elbow, following through. Players can practice this movement of the wrist with Wrist Snaps (see drill W14 on page 94).

One-knee arm circle

The player goes down on one knee and pitches to a target or catcher, focusing on keeping her shoulders back and her torso straight up and down as she releases the ball. Players can practice this circling movement with One-Knee Arm Circles (see drill W16 on page 95).

Half stride

When the player pushes off the rubber and lands, both of her feet are at a 45-degree angle and she is sideways to the catcher. The player starts at this spot in the pitching position and does a one-arm revolution, keeping her feet where they are but allowing them to pivot. Her hips will turn, but her feet will remain in place. Players can practice this movement of the feet in Half Strides (see drill W17 on page 95).

Half stride, finish with lower body

As the pitcher releases the ball, she pushes with her back foot and then brings it up to meet her front foot just slightly after the ball is released to the catcher. Players can practice this ending movement of the feet in Half Strides, Finish with Lower Body (see drill W18 on page 95).

The Mental Aspects of Pitching

Pitching is a high-visibility position, and some players are just better suited to the pressure than others. Players on both teams can become frustrated when the pitcher can't throw strikes; position players want strikes so the game can get moving, and batters want accurate throws so they can get a hit.

Talk with your pitchers. Set clear goals, and have them build up their stamina over time. Always have your pitchers warm up by throwing overhand, then begin practicing technique drills, and finally, practice the full pitching motion in incremental stages. I usually extend my pitchers' practice time by 10 minutes or so during each subsequent practice, but always be ready to recognize fatigue.

One of the difficult aspects of learning to pitch for some players is the idea that they might hit someone. Let your pitchers know that it probably will happen at some point, but that it's a part of the game, just like walks, strikes, and fly balls. Make sure the parents understand this too.

Batting

The Principles

Most of your players will love to bat, but all will have to bat. Batting is a complicated skill that can be broken down into four equally important components: the grip, the stance, the pivot, and the swing.

Grip

The bat should be held in the fingers, not in the palm. An indicator of the proper grip is having the second knuckles of both hands line up while holding the bat. The bat can be held firmer and deeper in the bottom hand. This may feel awkward at first for players who are used to gripping

Get a Grip! How to Hold the Bat

Most hitters should choke up on the bat an inch or so for better control. The better the bat control, the greater the swing speed. Here's how: With the bottom hand (lead arm), grip the bat like you would grip an axe. Then take the top hand and line your middle knuckles up between the second and third knuckles of the bottom hand. Do not grip the top hand on the bat as deeply or as firmly as the bottom hand, and remember not to squeeze the handle too tightly. The hands and forearm muscles should be relatively relaxed until the batter starts the swing forward.

Hold the bat with the fingers, not in the palm. Note that the second knuckles of both hands line up.

the bat back in their palms like a club, but it frees up the wrists tremendously and is crucial in developing a quick, compact swing and for increasing power.

Stance

Where a player stands in the batter's box isn't as important as finding that spot and standing there consistently. Each player should choose a spot in the box and always stand there so that pitches come to her in the same location every time. This will help her develop a routine for hitting. A good general guideline for establishing a batting stance is to put the back foot on the diamond shape of home plate and step into the box from there. Make sure she can cover the complete plate with her bat.

Pivot

Some players tend to let their toes "duck out," but it's very important that their toes and feet are straight or slightly "toed in." Their weight should be on the inside balls of their feet or on their two big toes. Their balance should be evenly distributed, their knees slightly bent.

     The key to powerful hitting is to remain balanced throughout the swing. Because younger players often have difficulty maintaining good balance during their swing, I recommend a "no stride" approach. In this approach, the player finds her starting position by standing in the box with feet shoulder width apart. She then strides out another 4–6 inches, so her legs are a bit farther apart than usual. This is the starting position. Her weight is on the inside balls of her feet, with her knees slightly bent. The player loads up and pivots on the balls of her feet without actually moving her feet. Her front foot pivots to open to a 45-degree angle.

     To "load up" means that when the player is balanced in her batting stance she rocks back and forth slightly to make sure her weight is evenly distributed. She then twists her body slightly away from the pitcher so that her weight and power are transferred (or "loaded") onto her back foot. This loaded-up power will be transferred into the swing as her body weight is transferred forward.

Loaded up. The batter has twisted her body slightly away from the pitcher so that her weight and power are transferred (or "loaded") onto her back foot.

Establishing the Proper Bat Angle

To establish the proper bat angle, the player should hold the bat in the proper grip and lay it on her shoulder so the bat is facing straight back. Then she lifts it up 2 inches off her shoulder, with the bat pointing directly behind—not curled around her head.

Matching Bat and Batter

A young hitter should use a bat that she can handle, which means a short, light bat. Swing speed, not bat weight, is key to hitting the ball far. Most young players are not physically strong enough to develop and generate a lot of rotational force, so until they reach approximately 13 to 14 years old, many players don't swing very efficiently. That's why a light, short bat is the key to a good, solid swing for young players.

Swing

Triggered by the inward turning of the rear knee and pushing off of the rear foot, the hips, shoulders, and body rotate explosively and quickly to the pitch. The rear foot pivots and the hips become square to the pitch. The wrists stay locked until the point of contact, when the player snaps and uncocks her wrists and hands. The top hand should be behind the bat at the point of contact. It is crucial that from the launch position to the point of contact the player's shoulders remain level and her hands snap to meet the ball. As her shoulders rotate through the swing, her head will start on the lead shoulder and end on the opposite shoulder; her head should otherwise remain as still as possible.

Always remind your players to keep their hands inside the path of the ball (between the body and the ball) as they move to it to swing. When players swing with their hands outside the line of the pitch, they swing more slowly and less effectively. Also remind them that in fast-pitch softball, the goal is a short, compact, powerful swing.

Bunting

Players bunt when you, the coach, give them the instruction to do so. This is usually done when the play is to advance a runner one base, either from first to second or second to third, by sacrificing the player who is batting via a fielder's choice to first. Although this is technically an "easy" play, it's usually not so

Uppercut: The Young Batter's Nemesis

The most common batting problem among young players is the dreaded uppercut. This term refers to a swing that follows an upward arc and often results in a pop fly or a strike. What causes an uppercut swing? When a player tries to pull the bat through the hitting zone with her arms, her rear shoulder droops along with her hands and the bat. From this low position, the bat starts its upward path to the ball, and the uppercut is born. Young players have this problem because the proper technique requires more strength and bat control. But they can do it. First, find a lighter bat. Then, work with them on developing quick hip and body rotation along with explosive use of the hands and wrists. The sequence of five hitting drills outlined in chapter 11 (see drills B1–B5 on pages 104–6) is designed to develop these skills, even in young players.

easy for young or developing players to correctly field a bunt. The sacrifice bunt can often result in the base runner advancing and in the batter reaching first safely.

The bunting batter stands in the batter's box closer to the front than the back in her usual batting stance. She then pivots to face the pitcher so that both feet are now pointing to the pitcher. She should move her feet slightly so that there is room between the two for optimum balance.

When the pitch is thrown, the player puts her thumb and forefinger of her top hand about halfway up the barrel of the bat, grips the handle with

The bunt: From the front of the box, the batter pivots to face the pitcher, waits for the pitch, and then "catches" the ball with a level bat.

Stress Individual Goals

When kids are developing their skills at batting and throwing, it is important to stress that they should work toward individual goals. There will always be some players who excel at hitting, and some who don't. You need to be careful that the players who aren't as proficient don't get discouraged because they aren't as good at certain skills as some other players. Rather than challenging your players to excel by saying, "Who can beat the team record with this drill?" make the challenge an individual one. Make sure every player is working toward a personal, realistic goal so that they all feel they are improving—working to accomplish something that is achievable for them.

Think about the Long Term

A difficult lesson for kids to learn is to forgo what feels good for the moment in favor of long-term benefits. This is important both on and off the field. When young players are learning new skills—or unlearning bad habits—the first outcome is a decline in performance. It's sort of a "one step forward, two steps back" progression. It's hard for kids to see the benefit of a new technique when they don't immediately play better than or even as well as they did before. In the long run, however, the progression ends up being "one step back, two steps forward," as the player learns and improves using new techniques.

The same is true off the field. It can be a real struggle for young players, especially as they reach adolescence, to make choices based on long-term goals rather than short-term gratification or pressure from their peers. But you can help them make choices that stress long-term success over immediate gain, making them stronger and more independent and confident young adults

the other hand, and pushes the bat in front of her face. She bends her knees (*not* the bat) to meet the ball and "catches" the ball with the bat. She "gives" when the ball reaches the bat to deaden the hit so that the ball travels only 10 to 15 feet from the plate. The bat angle stays level or slightly up throughout the bunt.

Baserunning

The golden rule of baserunning is to sprint to the bag. Often players wait to see where the ball goes, and if they think they won't make it to the base before the play is over, they jog slowly or just stop. Encourage your players to run as hard as they can every time the ball is in play. Even a good fielder can misjudge or misplay the ball, so what looks like an easy out may become a base hit.

When running to first base, players should hit the front edge of the base and run straight through the bag, stopping before they get to the grass. Then they peel around and get back to the bag, always ready to go to second on an overthrow. Players are not allowed to overrun second or third

Be Alert to Health Problems

There's nothing more frightening for a parent—or coach—than to see a child in distress and not know what to do. Breathing problems, including exercise-induced asthma, are more prevalent in children than ever before. Make sure that you talk to parents about how important it is for you to be aware of any preexisting physical condition that any of your players may have. In addition, parents need to give you as much information as possible about what to do if their child is in distress, and who to contact if problems occur. Forewarned is forearmed.

Most recreational leagues and schools will have health questionnaires and liability releases. If the league or school doesn't take care of this, ask parents to complete a brief questionnaire. This should alert you to potential major health issues. Having the league director review the questionnaire before you send it to parents could help make sure you ask all the necessary questions.

Above all else, the base runner should remember one thing: Sprint to the bag.

base. When running to second and third, a player should either should stop at the inside corner of the base or slide to the base.

It's important to be as efficient about the running movement as possible, so you'll want to work with your players to keep proper form: running on the balls of their feet, with elbows at right angles to their bodies as their arms pump, head moving as little as possible. Emphasize the piston action. Their arms should not be crossed over their chest. Remind your players to run in a straight line.

Minor Injuries? Think RICE

Bumps and bruises are a part of youth sports. If your player's injury needs more attention than the following, be sure to contact your local emergency room or physician. For minor sprains and strains, however, the RICE method will help a minor soft tissue injury heal faster.

- **Relative Rest.** Avoid activities that exacerbate the injury, but continue to move the injured area gently. Early gentle movement promotes healing.

- **Ice.** Apply ice to the affected area for 20 minutes; then leave it off for at least an hour. Do not use ice if you have circulatory problems.

- **Compression.** Compression creates a pressure gradient that reduces swelling and promotes healing. An elastic bandage provides a moderate amount of pressure that will help discourage swelling.

- **Elevation.** Elevation is especially effective when used in conjunction with compression. Elevation provides a pressure gradient: the higher the injured body part is raised, the more fluid is pulled away from the injury site via gravity. Elevate the injury as high above the heart as comfortable. Continue to elevate intermittently until swelling is gone.

When players are running around the bases, they should hit the inside front edge rounding first base and arc out around the other bases, running in as tight a circle as possible. Players should hit the inside corner of the bag with whatever foot comes up first—it doesn't matter if it's the right or left. They should lean toward the infield so their shoulders are at an angle toward the ground, keeping their momentum. Encourage your players not to loop beyond the bases, since they will be running a further distance than is necessary.

Players can't leave any base until the ball leaves the pitcher's hand. There is an 8-foot circle around the pitcher's plate called the *pitcher's circle*. When the ball is in the pitcher's circle, base runners must go in one direction or another or be called out, unless the pitcher makes a play on them.

Sliding

You can teach sliding fundamentals either on a sliding pad or on wet grass. There are two sliding techniques: the *bent-leg slide* and the *head-first slide* or diving slide. In the bent-leg slide technique, players should start sliding approximately 6–7 feet from the base. Keeping low to the ground, the player bends one leg and extends the other, gliding into the base on the calf, thigh, and buttocks of the bent leg. Her upper body should remain relaxed and extended back, and her arms, head, and hands should be up in the air to avoid a collision.

A head-first slide (left). Note the sheet for practicing. A feet-first slide (right). Hands are held high, and the knee is bent for protection.

In a head-first or diving slide, the player begins her slide approximately 6–7 feet from the base. Keeping low, she approaches the base and begins to lower herself to the ground while lunging forward, landing on her chest and belly evenly. Her head is always up and fingertips are either up in the air or in a fist. Her knees should not hit the ground first.

CHAPTER 5

The Practice

Preparation Is Key

The single-most important aspect of a successful practice is to *be prepared*. Make sure you come to practice with a complete plan for the entire practice—don't count on having any spare time to make plans just before practice starts, and don't decide to "play it by ear" and make up the practice as you go along. Write down your practice schedule and keep it handy so you can focus on teaching your players the proper techniques rather than worrying about what drills you should do next.

Be Early

Plan to arrive at practice between 15 and 30 minutes early. You'll need to set out equipment for your players, set up batting stations, and make sure the field is clear of equipment or obstacles that could pose a safety hazard. Often pitchers and catchers come to practice early to have extra time to

When warming up in the on-deck circle, players should always wear a helmet.

work on their skills. If you can't be half an hour early to the field for every practice, make sure that you are for the first one, in preparation for the meeting with parents and kids. This will give you time to introduce yourself and say a few words about your hopes and expectations for the season. It will also give you time to answer any questions parents or players may have.

Learn Your Players' Names

The first practice can be a very intimidating time for your players—and you. One way to keep things fun right from the start is to learn your players' names quickly and involve them in the process. The sooner you can learn and begin referring to them by their names, the sooner their confidence in themselves and their respect for you will grow. Gather your players together in a circle and have each player say her name. Explain to them that by the end of the practice you'll know each one of their names. Tell them that during practice you'll point to them randomly, and they should call out their names. After saying this, point to people in the circle and have them say their names so they get the idea.

Throughout the course of this first practice, stop everything every so often and point your finger at individual players to learn their names.

Remember Your Audience

When you are planning your practice session, follow the golden rule: *Keep it simple.* Don't assume your players know anything, and remember that younger children will need to have the same things repeated again and again until they understand it and remember it. You may find it helpful to draw the concept you are trying to explain in the infield dirt or on paper for players who don't understand. Always adjust your performance expectations to the age level you're coaching—a six-year-old has an entirely different level of body control and a much shorter attention span than will an 8- or 10-year-old.

The best way to keep things lively and fun is to use progressions of a skill by breaking the skill down into several components. Use shorter drills that players can move through quickly as they practice the same skill several different ways. Using stations during batting practice, for example, helps all the kids get involved at the same time and provides everyone with lots of repetition on basic fundamentals.

In general, always start practice with an activity that will be an easy success for your players. Work on the more difficult skill sets during the middle of the practice, and then end with something positive so they end practice on a positive note.

Practice Format

The following template is for a 90-minute practice session involving the whole team. Included in chapter 6 are practices for intermediate and

Help Them Learn to Listen

Telling your team to listen over and over will never be as effective as actually *training* them to listen to you. Talk to them about the importance of listening to you, and let them know that when you are talking you don't want others to be talking, and you want them to look at you. Then say that you are going to give them a test of their ability to listen. Tell them that when you clap and say, "Everybody up!" they should get up to begin practice. Explain what you will be doing that practice—running the bases, throwing, and working on infield/outfield drills. Then say, "Everybody up!" but don't clap. Half the team will jump to their feet while you just stand there or yell "Ah ha!" Let them figure out why some are standing and some are still sitting. Once they all sit back down, say, "I guess some of us weren't really listening." Then clap and yell "Everybody up!" and watch them all spring to their feet with their eyes and ears attuned to you. This is an effective way to get your players to realize that when you say you want them to listen to you, you really want them to *hear* what you have to say!

advanced players. These practices are scheduled for two hours and two and a half hours, respectively (see pages 65–70). Pitchers and catchers often practice a half hour or so longer than their teammates, to focus solely on pitching and catching skills. This can be done either before or after practice, depending on schedules. Chapter 6 includes sample pitching practices (see pages 70–71), and chapter 9 contains drills for both pitchers and catchers (see pages 94–97).

- Team meeting: 5 minutes
- Warm-up running and stretching: 10 minutes
- Throwing progression: 5 minutes
- Fielding fundamentals: 15 minutes
- Team defense: 10 minutes
- Batting practice: 30 minutes
- Scrimmages: 10 minutes
- End meeting: 5 minutes

Players should get to the field early. If they do not have specific skills on which they want to work in that extra time, give them something specific to work on. For example, never tell them to just throw. Rather, if they are outfielders, have them work on catching the ball with two hands, or if they are infielders, encourage them to develop their quickness in the transfer from the glove to hand to throw.

A Word about Safety

Never assume that your players will be aware of their own safety. Make sure that everyone begins and ends an activity at the same time, even during warm-up. This will help avoid accidents such as being hit with a thrown or batted ball. For more on safety, see the sidebars on pages 48 and 49.

Team Meeting (5 minutes)

Always begin practice promptly. Call your team in and let them know what specific skills you will be emphasizing that day and what areas in particular to work on. This meeting must be short (5 minutes maximum), lively, and full of anticipation. To help develop a team concept, end the meeting with a team cheer of some sort, such as "Let's go (your team name)!" and then start practice.

Warm-Up/Running and Stretching (10 minutes)

Unlike adults, kids don't need to spend much time warming up their muscles, and they usually don't have the patience to stretch for long. Instead, have them jog from one foul pole to the other foul pole, across the field and back. For older, more advanced players, you can increase the number of times they jog from pole to pole. Then have your players do some simple stretches as a team (see Stretching below). These should take only a few minutes.

Throwing Progression (5 minutes)

Throwing and catching are skills that your players will always need to practice. Spend at least 5 minutes (building up to 8 minutes) each day on these skills, and keep it interesting for your players by varying the drills you use.

Stretching

Hamstring and groin: Stand with legs as far apart as possible. Bend over at the waist and touch the grass. With all stretches, do them slowly without bouncing. Hold the position for a count of 5 to 10 seconds. Repeat, then swing over and touch left foot and then right.

Hamstring and lower back: Stand with feet together. Without bending knees, reach down and touch the grass, hold for a count of 5 to 10 seconds, and then slowly come back up to a standing position. Repeat.

Quadriceps: Stand with feet together. Lift one foot up so heel touches buttocks, holding the foot with one hand. Gently pull up on the foot so the quadricep muscle is stretched. Hold for a count of 5 to 10 seconds and repeat on other leg.

Groin and calves: Put feet as far apart as possible. Both toes face forward. Lean down to one side, bending knee and keeping feet flat on the ground. Hold for a count of 5 to 10 seconds, then repeat on the other side.

Shoulder girdle: Stand upright. Hold both arms out at a 90-degree angle. Swing each arm individually around one revolution, then switch arms.

Triceps: Stand upright. Reach back over the shoulder with one arm and try to touch as far down the middle of the back as possible. The other arm supports the elbow of the reaching arm.

Shoulder and deltoid: Stand upright. Reach one arm across the body so the front of the bicep is against the chest. The other arm pushes against the crossed arm to help stretch the shoulder and deltoid muscle. Switch arms.

Fielding Fundamentals (15 minutes)

In addition to throwing and catching, which are the most fundamental defensive skills, playing defense also involves a variety of specific skills that go together to create a foundation of proper mechanics. These include fielding with two hands, proper footwork, and body and hand positioning, to mention a few. While you need to introduce all of these fundamentals eventually, it's a good idea to focus on only one or two skills at a time. Remember that softball is a game where even the most elite players hone their skills on a continual basis, and it will certainly take more than one season for your players to master the basics.

Team Defense (10 minutes)

In this part of practice your team focuses on working out specific plays or situations that may occur during a game. The drills you choose to practice here will provide a game-like intensity for your players and allow them to practice at the positions they will most likely play during a game.

Batting Practice (30 minutes)

A common image of batting practice is one player hitting while 14 team-mates stand around watching. This isn't necessarily a good model. The key to keeping your players interested and learning is to keep everyone active and involved. At each batting practice, set up five separate defensive stations that your players will rotate through for 5 minutes each. Make it a game to

Fungoing to Players

Fungoes are simply balls hit for practice fielding by tossing a ball into the air and hitting it. They're a good way to teach your players proper fielding mechanics, and should be a part of every practice.

If you have trouble fungoing, first of all, practice. It may take time, but even coaches improve their skill at hitting practice balls as the season progresses. Secondly, use a toss that feels comfortable to you. Some coaches toss with their right hands, and some with their left. Either one is okay as long as your toss is high enough to allow enough time to get both hands on the bat, get your hands back, and swing comfortably. Also, make sure that your toss is not too close to your body. Allow for your arms to extend to the softball. Third, focus on using your hands. Primarily the wrists generate the power in your fungo swing, not your arms and shoulders. Fourth, watch the ball. See it meet the bat. Finally, adjust the arc of your swing for the type of ball you want to hit. In other words, swing slightly downward for a ground ball and slightly upward for a fly ball. But do not exaggerate these arc adjustments. If you err in any direction, err to the side of a level swing and effectively increase your margin for error.

If you find that your bat seems to have a hole in it, and that hitting the ball is not your particular strength—don't worry. Ask your assistant coach to do the hitting, or recruit a parent to perform the job. If that doesn't work, feel free to throw ground balls and fly balls. There is always a way. Don't let your own difficulties keep you from coaching or even from enjoying the process. After all, you don't have to be able to hit to encourage your players or to create an atmosphere of fun and strong effort.

The Discovery Method, Part 2

After you've explained a skill like throwing, ask one player at a time to repeat or show you what you've just taught them. This will also help players see that they need to pay close attention when you are teaching.

You can do this for each new drill and allow the drill to do the teaching. This will keep players attuned to what they are doing as they throw or catch or hit, and it will help them develop the ability to self-assess and articulate the mechanics that they are learning. Let your players use their own vocabulary to describe what they have taught themselves.

keep the rotation flowing quickly from station to station—keep the atmosphere focused, fun, and full of energy. This will be important, since without encouragement from you, players may have the tendency to stand around and talk rather than focus on their stations.

Ending Activity: Scrimmages (10 minutes)

This ending activity should be competitive and fun. You can emphasize the plays you want the team to work on, and the kids enjoy the game-like challenges. Mix it up each practice, keep this segment fresh and exciting, and always encourage players to win. Create small rewards or consequences for the winning and losing teams, but always in a light-hearted and positive way.

End Meeting (5 minutes)

Before your players go home, gather them together, congratulate them on their hard work, and point out things they did especially well. Now is the time to focus on specific players who have worked especially hard, or who have made solid improvement. Also give your players "homework," a skill that they can work on at home to become better players. This keeps them connected to the game and excited about showing off their improvement at the next practice.

Other Considerations

Softball is played and practiced outside under the sun in the hottest months. It's crucial that you schedule water breaks every 20 to 30 minutes during practice and have water available at the games. Kids should be encouraged to bring their own water bottles so that they get plenty to drink and to reduce the lines at the water fountain, but make sure the bottles have their names on them. Extreme heat can also be dangerous for young kids, so on very hot days give them a break during practice to sit in the shade and rest.

It's very important that kids are able to use the bathroom if they need to, sit in the shade if they feel overheated, or get your attention if they're hurt. Some kids can be very shy about these things. Make a point of addressing these issues at the first practice and let them know that they should speak up if a need arises. Then make sure that you listen.

Preparation is the single-most important factor in building successful practices. Always plan in advance. A practice worksheet, broken down into the different sequential segments, is an excellent planning tool.

Practice Session Worksheet

Team meeting (5 min.):

_____
_____
_____

Warm-up/running and stretching (10 min.):

_____
_____
_____

Throwing progression (5 min.):

_____
_____
_____

Fielding fundmentals (15 min.):

_____
_____
_____

Team defense (10 min.):

_____
_____
_____

Batting practice (30 min.):

_____
_____
_____
_____

Scrimmages (10 min.):

_____
_____
_____

End meeting (5 min.):

_____
_____
_____

Practice Session Worksheet

Sample of filled-out practice session worksheet.

Team meeting (5 min.):

Disuss carpool to Midland game Wednesday
Go over things we did well against
Panthers Tuesday — Talk about today's practice

Warm-up/running and stretching (10 min.):

Jog 1 lap
Stretch

Throwing progression (5 min.):

One-knee Throwing, Close
One-knee Throwing, Far

Fielding fundmentals (15 min.):

Diamond drill
Line fielding
Outfield run for infield

Team defense (10 min.):

Relay+entries

Batting practice (30 min.):

(split up group) dry swings
T-hitting
Hitting stations   Live hitting

Scrimmages (10 min.):

Controlled fungo

End meeting (5 min.):

Team cheer / Announcements

Developing this tone of accessibility is built on trust and approachability. They should feel that when they come to you with a problem or concern, you will listen respectfully and are willing to help.

Questions and Answers

Q. We've had only one practice, but we didn't get through even half of the recommended drills and practice segments. What should I focus on if I can't get through the whole thing?

A. Focus on the fundamentals. If you can teach your players to throw and catch well, you've taught them the keys to the game. Regardless of how much time you have to practice, always stress defense since you have to get outs to win the game. Team defense is fine, but fielding, throwing, and catching are the keys.

Q. I've had the good luck to get a group of kids who seem to really pick up the skills quickly. We've had two practices, and I've found that the kids are going through the blocks more quickly than the time I've allotted. They are getting bored, and I'm left with a big chunk of time at the end with nothing to do. How should I address this?

A. Always plan your practices with more material than you think you're going to need. Leave extra stuff at the end that you don't really need in case you don't get to it. Put the meat of the practice at the front, especially those skills that your players need to work on. Also, if they are moving too quickly through the drills you've assigned, make the drills more of a challenge: give your players more reps or longer distances, or turn the drills into mini-competitions so the kids are challenged on an individual basis.

The Position Checklist—From the Least to the Most Skilled

Every position on the diamond is important, and there's nowhere that a player can be concealed. In other sports there is always a concern that teammates will avoid passing the ball to a lesser-skilled player, but when the softball is hit to you or you are at bat, there's nowhere to hide. This is a good thing. But on the other hand, there are positions that are more central to the action. It's important that players get a chance to try all different positions, but don't hesitate to put your highly skilled players at the more skilled positions. The following list organizes the positions from least skilled to most skilled with respect to youth softball. At higher levels the first-base player may not be considered one of the more skilled positions, but at the youth level, where catching the ball is still a difficult task, first-base players are placed at a premium.

1., 2. (tie) Right field, Left field
3. Center field
4. Third base
5. Second base
6. First base
7. Shortstop
8. Catcher
9. Pitcher

Q. We've had three practices, and although the kids are enjoying themselves, they just aren't getting the skills. I've been trying to build on what we've done from the previous practice, but I feel like I have to keep reteaching the basics each time. Do I keep trying to move on, or just start all over again?

A. Always teach the basics. If your players' skill level hasn't developed, then pick a different drill to teach the same thing. Sometimes explaining or trying something in a slightly different way can make all the difference. You can add challenge to each skill by adding repetitions or a time limit, so that players who are progressing more quickly can be just as challenged as players who are taking longer to master the skills.

CHAPTER 6

Sample Practices

This chapter outlines three sample practices, covering all levels of play from beginner to more advanced. Watch your players carefully during practice to monitor their skill improvement. You may find that some or all of the players on your team excel at certain skills but need more work on others. You can adapt the drills to fit each player's abilities. As your team progresses in skills and experience, you can replace the drills outlined in these practices with other drills found in chapters 9, 10, and 11. You may find that if you are coaching a beginning team, you'll stay with the easy practice all season. That's fine, and by substituting other drills for the ones described here, every practice will be fun and exciting for your players.

Because softball pitchers need extra, individualized practice, included at the end of this chapter are three pitching-specific practices in addition to three sample full-team practices.

Basic Beginning Practice

This practice is great for all levels of play but is especially well suited for the youngest or least experienced players who are just learning the game. Older, more experienced players might benefit from this review during the first couple of practices. The emphasis here is on introducing and working on fundamental skills, with a focus on the basics of throwing, catching, pitching, fielding, and batting.

Team Meeting

Your first team meeting should be used to introduce yourself and your assistants (if you have them), to let your players know what you expect of them, and to learn their names (see page 53). At this first meeting, review or teach the fundamentals of throwing, catching, fielding, batting, pitching, and catching. Note players interested in pitching and catching, and make plans to meet with them either after the first practice to schedule individual sessions or at another, mutually convenient time. Show your players that you are excited and enthusiastic about the season ahead, and hope they are, too.

Warm-Up/Running and Stretching

The warm-up for every practice should consist of jogging between the foul poles and stretching (see Stretching, page 55) to get players loosened up and ready for action. Then players move into throwing and catching progression drills.

Throwing Progression

- **One-Knee Throwing, Close.** This drill emphasizes proper arm and body position when throwing, since it eliminates the lower body altogether. Have players do this drill without gloves, so they must catch with two hands, using softie balls or tennis ball. (See drill W2 on page 88)

- **One-Knee Throwing, Far.** Increase the distance between partners to approximately 25 feet. Players can use gloves and real softballs for this drill. Stress that they continue catching with two hands. (See drill W3 on page 89)

    To incorporate footwork technique into this drill, make sure players put their back feet perpendicular to the target and turn their bodies sideways before they throw.

One-Knee Throwing emphasizes proper arm and body position.

Fielding Fundamentals

These basic drills focus on good technique for fielding ground and fly balls. They can be used throughout the season and modified as your players become more proficient.

- **Two-Knees Fielding.** This drill helps players to have "soft hands" and to reach out when they field a ground ball. (See drill D1 on page 98)

- **Line Fielding.** This drill is a fast-moving way for players to practice their fielding skills. You and your assistant hit fungoes or roll balls for players to field. (See drill W10 on pages 91–92)

- **Quarterback Drill.** The goal of this drill is to help fielders become proficient at catching a ball hit over their heads. It is also great for conditioning and can be used for all positions. (See drill W9 on page 91)

Team Defense

Until your players are comfortable or familiar with the most basic skills, you shouldn't attempt to teach them specific defensive plays. However, once they can handle the basics of fielding and playing catch, they may be ready to practice some easy defensive plays.

- **Controlled Fungo.** All players, including the catcher, are in their positions. Extra players can be base runners during this drill. Put players at certain bases and call the play, such as "Runner on second, 1 out." Fungo the ball into play, and have your players react as if in a game situation. Either repeat the situation until your players master it, or play the inning out as if it were a game. You can also do this drill with just the infielders at their positions. (See drill D12 on page 103)

The Quarterback Drill will make kids comfortable about catching fly balls over their heads.

Batting Practice

For the batting segment of each practice, you'll need to set up beforehand five stations, far enough apart to ensure safety. Players will rotate around the stations at 5-minute intervals. The stations for this practice are as follows.

- **Single Tee Hits.** Players hit balls off the batting tee, starting with the tee as high in the strike zone as possible so they learn to hit high pitches first. (See drill B1 on page 104)

- **Soft Toss.** The batter hits softie balls into a net or out to an open space. The tosser is on one knee at a 45- to 55-degree angle to the batter, so when the tosser tosses the ball the batter won't hit the ball back at her. One partner tosses the ball underhand; the other partner swings. Halfway through the drill players switch places. (See drill B3 on pages 105-6)

- **One Knee, with Ball Hit off a Short Tee or Cone.** Players are on one knee, hitting the ball off a short tee. (See drill B9 on page 107)

- **Front Toss.** The coach tosses real softballs to players to hit. (See drill B4 on page 106)

- **Fast-Pitch with Real Softball.** The coach uses a screen or a Soft Toss position (see drill B3 on pages 105–6) to pitch to a player—it's even better if the coach can actually pitch the ball. The station is set up on the playing field, which helps give the batter a sense of a real pitching situation. Another option with this station is to have the player run it out and put a runner on first base. (See drill W20 on page 95)

A batting tee is an invaluable teaching tool. Use a fence or some other screen to save on ball chasing.

Ending Activity: Scrimmages

Ending activities should be competitive and fun. You can emphasize the plays you want the team to work on, and the kids enjoy the game-like challenges. Mix it up each practice, keep this segment fresh and exciting, and always encourage players to win. Create small rewards or consequences for the winning and losing teams, but always in a light-hearted and positive way.

The Controlled Fungo drill (see drill D12 on page 103) and the baserunning drills (see drills W11, W12, and W13 on pages 92–93) are good ways to end practices.

End Meeting

Bring your players together and recap the skills they worked on at this practice. Give them their homework for the next practice, such as making sure to use a two-handed catch. Encourage them to practice the techniques at home, and then remind them when and where their next practice will be. End with a cheer: "One, two, three, Team!" or something similar.

Intermediate Practice

With more advanced players, you can stress certain skill components in a particular practice that build on the basic fundamentals they have already learned. This intermediate practice is designed to take two hours. You may adapt it for your own time constraints.

Warm-Up/Running and Stretching

The entire team jogs between the foul poles four times and stretches (see Stretching, page 55). If pitchers and catchers have already been practicing, do not include them in the warm-up.

Throwing Progression

Pitchers and catchers should join in the regular practice at this time.

- **One-Knee Throwing, Close.** Follow the drill as described, but have players wear gloves and use real softballs. (See drill W2 on page 88)

- **One-Knee Throwing, Far.** (See drill W3 on page 89)

- **Stand Up and Throw.** Be sure to focus on the proper mechanics of throwing.

Fielding Fundamentals

Warm up your players' fielding skills by doing the following drills.

- **Diamond Drill.** This drill helps your fielders focus on quick lateral movement and good fielding position. Have your players do three sets of five tosses. (See drill W8 on pages 90–91)

- **Quarterback Drill.** Players do this drill by throwing to one side only, left or right, and then switch. (See drill W9 on page 91)

- **Line Fielding.** Do this drill from three stations: one third-base depth, one second-base depth, and one the depth of the outfield at center field. (See drill W10 on pages 91–92)

Team Defense

Try not to do too much teaching when your players are first learning these drills. Once they have the mechanics of the drill mastered, you can make teaching points. The following drills mimic game situations and give players the opportunity to think on their feet.

Coaching Your Own Child

Coaching when your child is on the team can either be the best or worst thing for the relationship, depending on how you handle the situation. The most important thing for you to do is to be as objective about your child's playing skills as possible. Be aware that she is bound to be scrutinized more closely than any other player by players and especially by their parents, so be extra vigilant to any tendencies that others may construe as favoritism. Remember, too, that it can be difficult for children to share their parents with other kids. Treat every child the same, including your own.

- **Infield Run for Outfield.** This drill is designed to work on defensive plays from the outfield. All of your outfielders play during this drill, taking turns making the plays. Infielders not playing defense can be used as base runners. The baserunning situations for this practice should be runner on first base only, then runners on first and second only. Fungo grounders and fly balls to the outfielders, who then make plays as if in a game situation. Each outfielder should have a chance to make 8–10 plays. (See drill D9 on page 101)

- **Outfield Run for Infield.** This drill reverses the players. Outfielders act as base runners while infielders play defense. Using the same baserunning situation as above, hit grounders and bunts to the infield to execute the defensive plays as if in a game situation. Allow each infielder to make 8–10 plays. (See drill D10 on page 101)

    If possible, your assistant can coach the base runners in this drill. This allows the players to work on their baserunning skills. Otherwise, players tend not to take baserunning seriously.

Batting Practice

Divide up your players into five groups. Each group will spend approximately 8 minutes at each station.

- **Single Tee Hits.** (See drill B1 on page 104)

- **Soft Toss.** One partner tosses a softie ball underhand; the other partner swings. (See drill B3 on pages 105–6)

- **Front Toss.** The batter is in the batter's box. The protective screen is approximately 15–30 feet out in front of the batter. You sit or stand directly behind the screen so only your arm comes out. Toss the ball and then duck behind the screen. Keep a bucket of balls handy. (See drill B4 on page 106)

- **Whiffle Toss from Front.** You, your assistant coach, or a player is 10–20 feet out in front of the batter on one knee. Pitch or throw the ball overhand into the pitching zone. You can use any size whiffle balls for this drill — for advanced players, you can use whiffle golf balls. The smaller the ball, the more challenging for the hitter. (See drill B10 on page 107)

- **Batting Practice with a Machine.** (See drill B7 on page 106)

Ending Activity: Scrimmages

Ending activities should be competitive and fun. You can emphasize the plays you want the team to work on, and the kids enjoy the game-like challenges. Mix it up each practice, keep this segment fresh and exciting, and always encourage players to win. Create small rewards or consequences for the winning and losing teams, but always in a light-hearted and positive way.

The Controlled Fungo drill (see drill D12 on page 103) and the baserunning drills (see drills W11, W12, and W13 on pages 92–93) are good ways to end practices.

End Meeting

Bring your players in and congratulate them for a good practice and a willingness to work toward improvement. Give them something to work on at home, depending on what seemed to need the most work during practice, and end with a team cheer.

Advanced Practice

This practice is designed to take up a 2-hour block of time. Pitchers and catchers should also practice together outside of this time allotment to hone their skills.

Warm-Up/Running and Stretching

The entire team jogs between the foul poles four times and stretches (see Stretching, page 55). If pitchers and catchers have already been practicing, do not include them in the warm-up.

Throwing Progression

This progression should be the same as that outlined for the intermediate practice, but add the following to the Stand Up drill.

- **Partner's Target.** The catching partner uses her glove to give a target to the throwing partner, varying the target every couple of throws. (See drill W7 on page 90)

Fielding Fundamentals

- **Diamond Drill.** Players perform three rounds of 10 tosses. (See drill W8 on pages 90–91)

- **Quarterback Drill.** Rather than throwing the ball always to one side and then the other, point to one direction and throw the ball over the player's other shoulder. This will force your players to watch the ball rather than anticipating the play. (See drill W9 on page 91)

- **Line Fielding.** Do this drill from three stations: one corner depth, one middle depth, and one outfield depth. The corners are first base and third base. Middle depth is second base and shortstop. (See drill W10 on pages 91–92)

Sliding/Diving Practice

These advanced fielding skills should be practiced only by those players who are skilled enough at fielding basics to accomplish the drill without injury. Half the players practice diving catches, and the others practice sliding; then the players switch. For sliding on grass, you can have the players remove their spikes. It's a good idea to practice sliding only on grass, not on dirt.

Team Defense

- **Outfield Run for Infield.** In this drill, use the situations of a batter bunting and runners at various multiple bases. (See drill D10 on page 101)

- **Controlled Fungo.** When the entire team takes part and extra players serve as base runners, this drill is as close to a game-like situation as any drill can be. Place runners at certain bases to begin the inning and allow the play to continue until the inning is over. (See drill D12 on page 103)

Batting Practice

Divide your players into five groups. Each group will spend approximately 8–10 minutes at each station.

- **Double Tee Hits.** Set up two batting tees with one in front of the other. When batters hit the ball off the back tee, that ball should then hit the ball off the front tee. Start with the tees close together and then move them apart as the players become more skilled. (See drill B2 on pages 104–5)

- **Bounce Toss.** The setup for this drill is the same as for Soft Toss (see drill B3 on pages 105–6), with the tosser at a 45- to 55-degree angle to the batter and the batter hitting into a net or open space. Bounce tennis balls into the hitting zone—this teaches the batter to have rhythm in her swing. (See drill B5 on page 106)

- **Soft Toss with Two Balls.** Follow the procedures for Soft Toss, using two balls. (See drill B3 on pages 105–6) Toss two balls, one right after the other, and call out which one to hit.

- **Two-Player or Four-Player Toss.** Players practice bunting in groups of two or four. With two players, one player tosses overhand to the other player, who bunts the ball. In the four-person version, a first-base player and third-base player field the balls. (See drill B6 on page 106)

- **Batting Practice with a Machine.** Use a double pitching machine if available and if your players' skill level warrants it. The machine pitches one high ball and one low, or one inside and one outside. (See drill B7 on page 106)

Ending Activity: Scrimmages

Ending activities should be competitive and fun. You can emphasize the plays you want the team to work on, and the kids enjoy the game-like challenges. Mix it up each practice, keep this segment fresh and exciting, and always encourage players to win. Create small rewards or consequences for the winning and losing teams, but always in a light-hearted and positive way.

The Controlled Fungo drill (see drill D12 on page 103) and the baserunning drills (see drills W11, W12, and W13 on pages 92–93) are good ways to end practices.

End Meeting

Bring your team in and tell them how pleased you are with the progress they have made and their hard work. If they have been winning a lot of games, warn them not to become complacent but to maintain their effort in practice and their energetic, fun spirit on the field. If they have been losing, let them know that softball is a tough game to learn and a real challenge to play. Encourage positive attitudes and end practice with a cheer.

Pitching Practices

Easy Practice (30 minutes)

This pitching practice is ideal for players just learning to pitch. Pitchers should warm up with a normal overhand throwing progression as outlined above.

All of the following drills are introduced in chapter 4 and more fully explained in Part 2, Drills.

- **Wrist Snaps.** The player should repeat the wrist-snapping motion with a ball approximately 25 times (5 minutes) (See drill W14 on page 94)

- **Elbow Snaps.** Repeat approximately 25 times (5 minutes) (See drill W15 on page 94)

Sports Creates Good People

One of the benefits of coaching children in sports is being able to provide opportunities for creating good people. Youth sports help influence character development even at a young age. Players can develop good citizenship practices through good sportsmanship and can learn to care for themselves and others, to take responsibility for their own actions, to strive for excellence, and to demonstrate integrity every time they step on the field. Showing respect for your opponents, taking pride in appearance during games, supporting other players and accepting responsibility for the outcome of games, good and bad, and working hard at practice and in games translate into life lessons that help shape children into the best people they can be.

- **One-Knee Arm Circles.** Repeat approximately 25 times (5 minutes) (See drill W16 on page 95)

- **Half Strides.** Repeat approximately 25 times (5 minutes) (See drill W17 on page 95)

- **Half Strides, Finish with Lower Body.** Repeat approximately 25 times (10 minutes) (See drill W18 on page 95)

Intermediate Practice (45 minutes)

- **One-Knee Arm Circles.** (5 minutes) (See drill W16 on page 95)

- **One-Knee Double Arm Circles.** (5 minutes) In this drill, the pitcher should make two arm revolutions, focusing on the speed of the motion. (See drill W19 on page 95)

- **Half Strides, Finish with Lower Body.** (5 minutes) (See drill W18 on page 95)

- **Learn a Pitch.** (5 minutes) The pitcher combines the Half Strides drill (see drill W17 on page 95) with ball spins 15 feet out from the pitching rubber. The player should work from a half-stride position, spinning the ball off her hand rather than following through with the pitch.

- **Throw a Pitch.** (15 minutes) The pitcher follows through with the pitching motion from full distance. (See drill W21 on page 96)

- **Throw Fast Balls to the Four Corners of the Plate.** (10 minutes) (See drill W22 on page 96)

Advanced Practice (45 minutes)

- **Half Strides.** (5 minutes) (See drill W16 on page 95)

- **Full Pitch Fast Balls to Four Corners of the Plate.** (10 minutes) The setup for this drill is the same as for the Throw Fast Balls to the Four Corners of the Plate drill (see drill W22 on page 96). In this drill, the pitcher is working on her speed and control.

- **Work on Alternating Pitches.** (30 minutes) Players alternate between pitching a drop ball and a fast ball or between a change up and a fast ball. (See drill W23 on page 96)

CHAPTER 7

Game Time

The Mental Aspect

The first game of the season can be both exciting and intimidating. You may find that you are more nervous than your players. This is the first time that all your players' hard work will be put to the test, and your coaching skills will be put to the test as well. Remind yourself—and your team—that while it is easy to judge how good you are by the end score, one team has to win and one has to lose. It's up to you to recognize and promote the process of the game rather than its outcome.

Scoring Position

If you listen to a baseball announcer on TV or the radio, or if you hang around softball coaches for very long, you might hear someone say something about "runners in scoring position." What are they talking about? Obviously, anyone who is on base or even at bat is in scoring position, meaning they have the potential of scoring at any moment. But when people refer to runners in scoring position they mean that the runners are capable of scoring on a single. The players who are within range of scoring should a single be hit are those who are on either second or third base.

Set an Example

The most important role you'll play in the game will be as an example to your players. No matter how much you talk to your players about being good sports and showing respect for the game by showing respect for others, your actions will speak much more vividly than your words.

Always treat the umpires with the respect they deserve. If you have a question about a call, wait until the play is dead; then approach the umpire and talk to him or her calmly. You will certainly experience bad calls from time to time—at this level, umpires might be high school students, parent volunteers, or other inexperienced officials. But even at the elite level, bad calls are made, and you will need to accept this with grace and move on. If an umpire exhibits inappropriate behavior, you should address it with his or her superior at a different time.

Never tolerate comments from parents or players to umpires—you are the only person who should address the umpires in any way. Let your players know that if there is a question about a call or a call goes against them, one of the things they need to learn is that they have to deal with adversity. Officials are part of the game, and they are doing the best job they can.

Look the Part

Part of setting a good example as a coach is looking the part. Before game day, meet with your assistants and agree to a coaches' "uniform," an outfit that complements your players' uniforms and makes you look neat and part of the team. Coaches who dress like slobs or show up at games wearing T-shirts that advertise beer or have other inappropriate slogans are not setting an example their players should emulate. Unlike baseball coaches, most elite-level softball coaches wear casual clothes such as khaki shorts, a polo shirt, and softball or tennis shoes.

Know the Rules

By game day you should have a working knowledge of the rules of the game in general and of your league in particular. Each league may have a different set of rules regarding pitching distances, whether there will be a certain number of walks allowed per inning, whether all players must be in the field and bat at least one inning, if the game will be limited by time or innings, and so on. These rules are important to learn, since they may well affect your substitution policy; if you base your player rotation on a policy of six-inning games, and the league's rules are that games must end by 7:30 P.M, some of your players may not have the chance to play at all.

Establish Team Protocol

Your team should be familiar with your game philosophy well before they step onto the field on game day. If you've decided your policy will be that everyone on the team plays every game, stick with it, regardless of the action on the field. The minute you change your philosophy to react to what's happening on the field, you immediately lose credibility with your players.

Be Prepared

Have a plan prepared for the game just as you would for practice. The plan should include making sure the necessary equipment is accounted for and at the field, a pregame practice routine, a starting lineup, and a substitution schedule. Also make sure before you leave home that you bring a first-aid kit, including ice packs. The home team usually furnishes game balls, but make sure that you have a few in your equipment bag as well, just in case.

Plan a half-hour pregame warm-up that focuses on fundamental skills. For older players, include team defense drills in the warm-up.

Plan Your Substitution Pattern

Player substitution is an important issue and should be planned out ahead of time. Depending on your league's rules, if a player is taken out of the game, she may or may not be allowed to come back in. Once again, how you handle the situation will depend on the age of the players.

You should flip-flop the players who start and the players who finish each game so the same players don't always play the first three or the last three innings of every contest. Also, try to arrange combinations of players that

---

Running It Out

As a coach, you want to instill in your players an attitude of hard work and good hustle. One of the most obvious signs of a team that has been coached to work hard and to hustle is one that sprints all-out after hitting a ball. Don't let your players adopt the habits of many major leaguers who are often guilty of jogging to first base after grounding the ball to an infielder. Your players should sprint through first base, regardless of where the ball is hit. No play should be assumed an automatic out, for good things happen to those who hustle. The same goes for fly balls. If the ball is hit high in the air, challenge your players to sprint for second base just in case the ball is dropped. What a joy it is to see young players playing the game with energy and respect. Congratulate them for their hustle and self-discipline and let them know how good it looks.

will work well together. In general, you want to have your strongest players "up the middle"—meaning at catcher, pitcher, shortstop, second base, and center field—and at first base for younger players. Obviously, this will not always be possible, but playing your more skilled players at these positions often makes a very difficult game progress more smoothly for everyone on the field. By strategically placing skilled players in a few of these positions, the game can be more fun and a better learning experience for your entire team. However, don't confine players to certain positions if they have aspirations to play elsewhere. Give them the opportunity to play a variety of positions.

Batting Order

You'll also need to establish a batting order for each game that allows players to hit in different spots in the lineup each game. Very simply, you can use the position numbers—1 through 9—to create a rotating pattern. For the first game, bat through the order from 1 to 9, or in other words, from the pitcher to the right fielder. Begin the second game with 9, 1, 2, 3, . . . and the third game with 8, 9, 1, 2, 3, . . . Then, when you substitute for a player, the new player will simply fill in the appropriate spot in the batting order.

Meet the Other Coach and Umpires

Before the start of every game, make a point of walking over and introducing yourself to both the opposing coach and the umpire. It helps to put a friendly face on the contest and shows your players that you respect the umpire and the other team. Also be sure to ask the umpire to go over any ground rules (exceptions or special circumstances specific to the ballfield, such as "a ball is foul if it hits the branches overhanging the foul line in right field"). You'll be glad you did if something unusual happens during the game.

Coaching the Game

The Start of the Game

Immediately before the game starts, bring your players together. Offer them a few words of encouragement and remind them that the reason they are here is to have fun, be respectful of others, and do their best. Also give them a specific goal to work on, such as making sure they catch with two hands. This will take some of the focus off winning or losing as the only goal toward which to work. Setting small, concrete goals within a game is a good way for players to remember that strong fundamental skills are especially important.

Have a team cheer to get your players fired up. Then, if you're the home team and are starting on defense, players who are starting on the field should sprint to their positions, ready to play. Players on the bench should sit down and be ready to cheer for their team. If you begin the game on offense, your first batter should put on her helmet and head toward the plate, while the on-deck batter warms up. Players on the bench should sit in

The Hero or the Goat: Winning and Losing with Grace

There will be days when your team is the hero and days when it is the goat. If you stay in the sport long enough, you'll experience them both—usually sooner rather than later. When you are the goat, you always remember how it felt.

It is important to keep winning and losing in perspective: either your team played better that day, or the opposing team did. Young players will likely have many opportunities to experience winning and losing, but as coach, you should help them concentrate on the process, not the outcome. I still remember times when people rubbed their victory in our faces and I remember players and coaches who won with dignity and mutual respect. Focus on how your team played, not just the score. And show your players, by example, how to be gracious winners and losers.

the order they will bat, with the first player after the on-deck batter at the end of the bench closest to the plate.

Chatter

Whether your team is on offense or defense, your players should "talk it up" for their teammates. Players on the field and on the bases need encouragement, and it helps to keep kids on the bench in the game as well. Make sure that your players know you won't tolerate any inappropriate comments or derogatory words by any member of your team. Encourage your players to be supportive of the pitcher and of players who make mistakes on the field. Remind players on the bench that positive comments are the only kind you should hear.

Many parents and coaches who are new to the sport may be surprised to hear softball players "singing" their cheers. For some reason, this is a long-standing tradition in fast-pitch softball. Some cheers can be long and elaborate while others are shorter. Either way, the songs/cheers should be designed to cheer for your team and not against your opponent.

Third-Base Coaching

When your team is at bat, you or your assistant become the third-base coach, who is responsible for giving signs or instructions to the batter and runners, reminding players of the number of outs, and instructing runners rounding second and third bases. The instructions you'll give include signaling them to round a base and continue on to the next one, to stay at a base, or to slide. If you want a runner to continue on to the next base, signal it by circling your left arm like a windmill. If you want her to stay at a base but not to slide, hold both of your arms and hands up. And if you want a player to slide, energetically wave and point your arms toward the ground and call, "Down!" Don't be afraid to be aggressive on offense—throwing someone out from the outfield is very difficult because it requires a good throw, catch, and tag, all put together. Encourage your players to take chances baserunning.

When giving signals to the batter, keep them few and simple. Most of the time the batter is just trying to hit the ball safely (as in get a hit).

When Nothing Is Going Right

You'll have games when it seems like your players can't get out of their own way. This is the time to get in a huddle and remind everyone of the process of the game, rather than the outcome. Give them specific goals to work on every inning—such as playing catch well, communicating as a team, and getting outs. This takes the emphasis off how many runs you or the other team has. This helps you control the things you can. If your team can't seem to hit, tell them their goal for the inning is to be aggressive and swing at first pitches. If they're having trouble catching the ball, make the goal for the next inning to always catch with two hands. Always be encouraging, have a sense of humor, and keep the atmosphere positive.

Taking Stock

After each game is a good time to assess where you are and where you want to be. It can be tempting to focus entirely on the number of runs scored and to concentrate solely on your win-loss record as indicators of how the team is doing: if you are winning games, the season is going great; if you're losing, the season is going poorly. Rather than allowing game scores and team records to dictate the status of your season, remember that the whole point of coaching your players is to help them have fun and enjoy learning to play softball.

Games will usually be a good test of a team's strengths and weaknesses. Use games as vehicles for evaluating progress in skill development and in how well your players are coming together as a team. Although individual and team skill development is important, the first and most impor-

Softball: A Game of Numbers

Softball is a game of numbers. Every aspect of the game—fielding, pitching, batting, baserunning, you name it—can be recorded. These statistics can be helpful for you to use as a way of showing your players the areas in which they are strong as a team and the areas on which they need to work. If you choose to share the stats with your players, use them to challenge and encourage your team, and never to discourage. For example, you may say in practice, "We had 12 hits and stole 4 bases last game—signs of a healthy and aggressive offense—but we had some defensive problems." Without saying that your team committed 14 errors, you can challenge them to focus on defensive work in practice and still keep the atmosphere positive. But on the other hand, it is important to discourage individual players from becoming concerned with their own personal stats. A group of players becomes a team when it disregards individual pursuits and glory. And a team has fun when it finds joy in collective accomplishment. Players focusing too much on personal statistics can destroy a good team-first attitude.

tant question you should ask is, "Are the players having fun?" The second question should be, "Are the players improving individually?" Make a checklist of the different skill areas and assess how your players are developing and progressing in these skills. The skill areas include:

- Catching fly balls and throws around the infield
- Throwing accuracy
- Fielding ground balls
- Aggressive batting
- Sprinting around the bases regardless of the situation
- Keeping chatter consistent and positive
- Playing with energy and enthusiasm

Remember that for most young players, it all comes down to fundamentals, fundamentals, fundamentals. Work on the basics—the team that plays catch the best is the team that makes the most successful plays on the field. Save complicated plays for when your players can catch and throw the ball with ease and confidence. When they are ready, begin with a few simple plays and increase the variety and complexity. And when in doubt, go back to the basics again.

Questions and Answers

Q. I have eight kids who want to play shortstop—I want them to play where they are excited to play, but clearly all of them can't play the same position. What should I do?

A. You have enthusiastic players? Great! Script out their playing time, either game by game, or inning by inning. They'll know when they get to play, and everyone will know it's a fair way to divide up playing time. Encourage your players to try as many different positions as possible so they get a sense of the whole field.

Softball: A Humbling but Great Game

Good softball players play the game hard and have great respect for the game, their coaches, and their teammates. Young players need to understand how difficult it is to play and learn the game—and to realize that it takes a lifetime of practice to hone their skills. No matter how good you think you are, at each level, on a given day, the game can humble you. Learn from past mistakes, but think about the next pitch, the next at bat, the next opportunity. Have a team-first attitude. Do what you can to help the team win. Take pride in your team, your teammates, and your own play. Softball can be a frustrating game, but the game can also give you great pleasure and satisfaction. There will be adjustments and new challenges at each level. Take a lot of personal pride in what you've learned and accomplished and look forward to the next challenge.

Q. I made it clear that I expected my players to respect the umpires and their decisions, but the ump we had at the first game was terrible and clearly didn't know some of the rules of the game. I didn't say anything at the time, but after the game my players had questions about the rules and the umpire. What do I tell them?

A. If the ref was really bad, alert the league office after the game that the quality of refereeing wasn't appropriate for the skill level being played. If your players have a question, openly and honestly talk to them about it. Let them know that people make mistakes, but that's the way it goes sometimes, and there will be times when your team won't get breaks. Continue to stress the importance of good sportsmanship to your players, regardless of the situation.

Q. We won our first game, and after it was over some of my players were whooping and shouting. I was glad they were excited, but how much celebrating after a win is too much?

A. Several minutes after a game, while your team is still together, it is fine to cheer. Be sure to end the celebration before lining up and shaking hands with the other team.

Q. Our team lost in a huge way. The kids worked hard and played well, but we were simply outmatched. They are feeling very low—how can I get them back on track and excited again?

A. It's important to teach your players how to win—and lose—with class. The best way to do this is to stress the process of the game, not its outcome. Winning is a bonus of a game played well, and losing is a disappointment, not a crisis. After each game, go back over the process of the game and the goals you had for it and assess what your players accomplished during the game. Give credit for things they did well, and point out things they need to work on. There will be days when they play terribly and win, or play well and lose. By stressing the process, winning and losing will be put in better perspective. If you don't overcelebrate winning along the way (see previous question) and assess the process goals after each game, win or lose, getting over losses is much easier.

CHAPTER 8

Dealing with Parents and Gender Issues

Parents are the most enthusiastic supporters of youth sports you'll find anywhere. They come to games, regardless of the weather, bake dozens of cookies, hold raffles and fund drives, and cheer loudly for their kids' teams, no matter how lopsided the score. Parents are such strong supporters of their kids, in fact, that you may find that they want to do more than just cheer the team; they may want to "help" you coach, too. This can be a big problem if it isn't addressed right away at your parents' meeting, in a letter, or at the first practice.

The Role of the Parents

The Golden Rule for Parents: Support the Coach without Actually Coaching

A little softball (or any sports) knowledge can be a real pain for a coach — it is very difficult to have a parent who chips away at your authority and coaching skills because he or she "knows a thing or two" about the sport. You need to be perfectly clear from the beginning that the role of parents should be to support the team by supporting you. Make sure that you and all of the parents on the team are in clear agreement with your philosophy and methods before the season starts, especially if you are in a competitive league (a competitive league inevitably means competitive parents). If you are aware of the abilities of other teams versus your own, go over the season schedule with parents so they can be prepared for difficult games and won't second-guess your decisions or commitment to play everyone, regardless of the score, when the game is on.

It's important to point out to parents that every comment, even those that their kids overhear at the dinner table, can have an effect on their children's attitudes.

During practices or games, the best place for parents is in the stands,

It isn't about winning. Let your players have fun, and they'll remember the experience fondly.

Let Parents Know the Risks

Because softball can be a sport conducive to injury, make sure that parents know the risks and dangers. Broken noses and fingers, scrapes and bruises, are very common in softball, and parents should know this at the outset.

far enough back from the team bench and field so that they can be supportive from a distance. Part of the reason for this is team-based: it's important that when kids come off the field during a game, they are focused on being part of a team, rather than being an individual. If things haven't gone well, they shouldn't be able to go off the field to their parents for consolation (or criticism)—they've got to be consoled within the team, with the coach, and with each other.

The very best thing parents can do for their children is to take the responsibility of being a team member seriously: get their kids to practice and games on time, make sure all parts of the uniform and all equipment are ready for the game, and provide as much positive support and encouragement as possible.

Winning Isn't the Only Thing

Like you, the parents of your players need to keep winning and losing in careful perspective—they have to be above caring too much about whether their children win or lose games, since their kids will care so much. Parents also need to be comfortable with the playing time their children get on the field and to trust you to be fair and substitute players appropriately.

Let Parents Voice Their Opinions

You don't need a special meeting to get feedback from parents—make it clear that you have an "open door" policy where they are welcome and encouraged to talk with you about how things are going, as long as it is in an appropriate time and place. You will certainly need to set the parameters for communication. One great way to get feedback from parents is through social events such as postgame cookouts or picnics. You give them the opportunity to tell you what's on their mind in a nonconfrontational environment, and you'll pick up some great information about your season and your team.

Get Parents Involved

The more you can get parents involved in off-field activities surrounding your team, the better. If you have a parent who is coordinating other administrative duties, he or she can help organize off-field activities as well, such as fund-raising, carpooling, and cookouts. Parents want to be a part of their children's lives, and this is an ideal way to do it.

Gender Issues

At the youth level (under 12), boys and girls have almost identical levels of athletic ability. The drills in this book are appropriate for either girls or boys, although there are far more girls participating on softball teams than boys, and thus the drills are designed primarily for girls. As boys reach teenage years and, on average, develop greater upper-body strength, some modification of drills may be necessary.

Some variance in coaching style may also be necessary for coaches used to working with boys. Girls tend to take criticism very personally, and they are usually more open to doing whatever is asked without knowing the rationale behind a particular drill or skill. You won't have to change your coaching philosophy if you're coaching girls for the first time. Just be prepared to offer them a bit more direction. You'll find that girls are every bit as competitive as boys and often more coachable. Negative or harsh comments will not bring out that competitive spirit in girls, but a positive and supportive coaching style will.

Also remember that unlike most sports, softball doesn't give girls many role models to emulate. They come to the sport with no expectations or preconceptions about what they "should" be doing, and thus they are extremely receptive to coaching. The longer girls have fun in a sport and are challenged by it, the longer they tend to participate. When girls can no longer succeed in a sport, they quit. Your most important goals as a coach are to help foster success in your players, help keep the game fun for them, and help keep them involved in sports for as long as possible.

Questions and Answers

Q. I have some parents who keep giving their kids "advice" after games and practices about their performances that I really disagree with. How do I address this?

A. The best way to deal with this without interfering with the relationship between parents and children is to make it clear at the beginning of the season that while the players are on the field, you are the coach. If parents want to give advice or tell their children what to do off the field, that's up to them. However, when players are on the field during practice or games, you should be the only person in charge, and your voice is the only one the players should listen to. Make that clear to the parents if it is an issue.

Q. Some parents insist on sitting right behind the bench and make comments during the game about the other team and the refereeing. I know they are trying to be supportive to the kids and the team, but I don't like it. What's a diplomatic solution here?

25 Benefits of Playing Sports

The Women's Sports Foundation compiled the following list of benefits that girls can achieve from their participation in sports. The list confirms the importance of maintaining girls' interest in sports.

1. Sports are FUN!
2. Girls and women who play sports have a more positive body image than girls and women who don't participate.
3. Girls who participate in sports have higher self-esteem and pride in themselves.
4. Research suggests that physical activity is an effective tool for reducing the symptoms of stress and depression among girls.
5. Playing sports teaches girls how to take risks and be aggressive.
6. Sport is where girls can learn goal-setting, strategic thinking and the pursuit of excellence in performance and other achievement-oriented behaviors—critical skills necessary for success in the workplace.
7. Playing sports teaches math skills.
8. Sports help girls develop leadership skills.
9. Sports teach girls teamwork.
10. Regular physical activity in adolescence can reduce girls' risk for obesity.
11. Physical activity appears to decrease the initiation of cigarette smoking in adolescent girls.
12. Research suggests that girls who participate in sports are more likely to experience academic success and graduate from high school than those who do not play sports.
13. Teenage female athletes are less than half as likely to get pregnant as female non-athletes (5% and 11% respectively).
14. Teenage female athletes are more likely to report that they had never had sexual intercourse than non-athletes (54% and 41%).
15. Teenage female athletes are more likely to experience their first sexual intercourse later in adolescence than female non-athletes.
16. High school sports participation may help prevent osteoporosis.
17. Women who exercise report being happier than those who do not exercise.
18. Women who exercise believe they have more energy and felt they were in excellent health more often than non-exercising women.
19. Women who are active in sports and recreational activities as girls feel greater confidence in their physical and social selves than those who were sedentary as kids.
20. Women who exercise miss fewer days of work.
21. Research supports that regular physical activity can reduce hyperlipidemia (high levels of fat in blood).
22. Recreational physical activity may decrease a woman's chance of developing breast cancer.
23. Women who exercise weigh less than non-exercising women.
24. Women who exercise have lower levels of blood sugar, cholesterol, triglycerides and have lower blood pressure than non-exercising women.
25. Regular exercise improves the overall quality of life.

Reprinted with permission from the Women's Sports Foundation, <www.WomenSportsFoundation.org>. For full citations of the research cited above, please contact the Foundation at 1-800-227-3988 or wosport@aol.com.

A. This is where the preseason letter becomes so important. Be clear in that note about the expectations for coaches, players, *and* parents regarding good sportsmanship. Explain that softball is a chance to teach kids the skills of the game and, more importantly, important lessons on respect, discipline, and positive behavior. Then, if the situation with a parent becomes out-of-hand, you can discreetly point out to them the importance of modeling sportsmanship to the kids.

Q. I have a parent who constantly questions my judgment about how much time each team member plays. This parent feels that his child, who is quite good, is not playing enough. I have explained that it is important for every team member to play, regardless of ability. We simply don't see eye-to-eye on this, and the parent cannot accept my explanation.

A. At the first meeting of the season with both parents and players, ask the kids whether they would rather play and possibly lose a game, or sit on the bench and win. Inevitably, the kids will opt to play the game, and the parents, standing behind the kids, are witnesses to the fact that the players themselves want equal playing time. Let it be known at that point, to both the parents and kids, that you will schedule equal playing time for each team member, regardless of the game situation. No parent, then, can argue during the season that his or her child should be playing more than any other. You and the kids themselves endorse the equal playing time rule, a rule to which you will remain consistent. Also remind parents that there are more competitive leagues out there, and if playing to win is more important than anything else, they are sure to find another team that has the same philosophy.

PART TWO

Drills: The Foundation for Development, Success, Happiness, and a Coach's Peace of Mind

Warm-Up: Throwing, Fielding, and Baserunning Drills and Drills for Pitchers and Catchers

Throwing Drills

Basketball Spins W1

Purpose: To teach how to snap the wrists when throwing the softball, rather than pushing it. Ideally, the ball should rotate many times through the air.

On one knee (or standing), players put the ball up overhead as if to shoot a basket and spin it in the air using a wrist snap. The ball rotates through the air off the fingers. Players get used to the feel of their wrists snapping and the ball rotating off the fingertips, not the palm of the hand.

Basketball Spins will give players the right feel for releasing the ball.

One-Knee Throwing, Close W2

Purpose: To break down the throwing motion. Players are on one knee to concentrate on upper body position and movement.

Players are paired with a partner and are 15–20 feet apart. One player brings the ball back behind her so it is at a 90-degree angle at her armpit and elbow. The ball is turned away from her and faces the opposite direction from her target. From this position, the player's elbow comes forward high up along the ear and moves forward like an overhand serve in tennis. The player releases the ball in a throw to her partner and lets her hand relax, following through down to her waist. The glove hand should point toward her target so her shoulders open and turn sideways to the target as she throws, rotating her torso. Players do the drill without a glove so they must catch with two hands. Use softie balls or tennis balls.

One-Knee Throwing, Far W3

Purpose: To focus on proper arm and body position when throwing.

Players throw to a partner as in One-Knee Throwing, Close (see drill W2 page 88), but this time the distance between them increases to 25 feet. Players wear gloves and use real softballs but continue to use two hands for catching.

Throw to Partner's Target W4

Purpose: To practice accurate throwing and catching.

Players give a target to a partner when they throw back and forth. The throwing player should work on proper throwing technique, as in One-Knee Throwing, Close and One-Knee Throwing, Far (see drills W2 and W3). The player who receives the ball should move her body so that she catches the ball in front of her body, rather than moving her glove to the side.

Around-the-Horn Throwing W5

Purpose: To build teamwork, hone throwing and catching skills, and simulate catching and throwing situations in the game.

Players line up three or four across at each base, including home. The first players in line work the ball around the bases, beginning at home, with a throw to first, second, and third, trying to complete as many consecutive throws as possible. Have all the players count each throw out loud. After a drop, the next players in line step up. Players should work on proper throwing and catching techniques. As players become comfortable with this drill, they should switch direction.

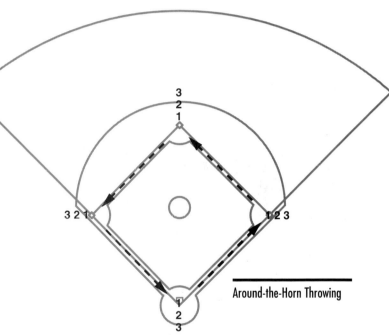

Around-the-Horn Throwing

Long Toss W6

Purpose: To build players' stamina and arm strength over time.

Players throw a ball to a partner and then take a step backward. Gradually they work their way backward to a distance as far as they can throw with good technique and accuracy. Players should then throw 8–10 times at this distance. At no time should mechanics of the throw break down. Throws should be strong, smooth, line drives, not high arcs. If a player needs to make high, blooping throws to reach her partner, the players are too far apart.

Partner's Target W7

Purpose: To work on throwing and catching accuracy.

Players take partners and spread out between 20–25 feet apart. The catching partner uses her glove to give a target to the throwing partner, varying the target every few throws.

Fielding Drills

Diamond Drill W8

Purpose: To hone lateral movement and create "quick feet" when a player is trying to get the ball. This drill and the Quarterback Drill (see drill W9 on page 91) are the two most fundamental drills for fielding footwork.

Players take partners. Based on their field positions, the partners stand approximately 5 feet apart (first- and third-base players) or 10–15 feet apart (middle infielders and outfielders). One player in each group is on her knee, facing her partner. She rolls the ball slowly on the ground to her partner's left or right. The receiving partner shuffles her feet (not crossing them) and, staying down, bends her knees. She fields the ball and lightly tosses it to her partner. The throwing player then throws to her partner's other side.

Variation: As players become more proficient at this drill, have them use two balls. The throwing partner rolls the first ball to the receiving player. As soon as the receiving player touches the first ball, the throwing player rolls the second ball to the player's other side. The fielding player should remain in the crouched position at all times.

Quarterback Drill W9

Purpose: To help players in all positions learn to catch balls thrown or hit over their heads. This drill also teaches players how to drop-step (step back and then take a step to the side), turn, and run for fly balls.

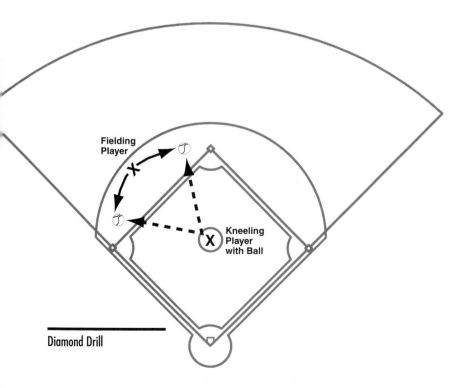

Fielding Player

Kneeling Player with Ball

Diamond Drill

Players perform this drill in the outfield, away from any obstacles on the field.

Players line up facing the coach. Each player has a ball and gives it to the coach when it is her turn. The player faces the coach, who is approximately 5 feet away. The coach points in the direction she will throw the ball, either to the left or right of the player. The player drop-steps, turns, and runs straight back, looking back by turning only her head to see the ball. The coach tosses the ball over the player's shoulder so the player has to reach to catch it. The player runs back to the end of the line. Two coaches and two lines of players can perform this drill at the same time.

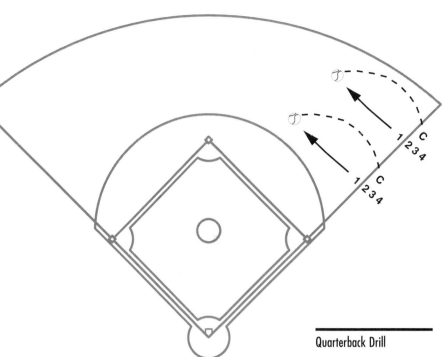

Quarterback Drill

Variation: To make this drill more difficult, the coach points in one direction but throws the ball to the other side, making the player have to take her eye off the ball while she turns her head to pick up the ball on the other side of her body, without breaking stride.

Line Fielding Drill W10

Purpose: To improve basic fielding skills. If you have more than one person able to hit fungoes, you can have this drill take place in various areas of the field.

Divide your players into groups of three or four, depending on how many people are available to hit fungoes. Line your players up at three depths: third-base depth (i.e., the person hitting fungoes should stand as far from the line players as the distance from home to third base), second-base depth, and the depth of the outfield at center field. Each area will have a person who hits fungoes to the first fielder in line. Have each group of players bring a bucket or bag with them to collect the balls they field.

The coach or assistant hits one fungo to each fielder, who fields the ball with proper fielding mechanics, puts the ball in the bucket or bag, and goes to the end of the line. Each fielder should have three or four turns at each fielding station before moving to the next. They then bring the bucket back. This drill allows players to get a lot of repetition at fielding without doing much throwing.

Variation: Have fielders throw the balls back to the batter rather than collecting them in a bucket or bag.

Baserunning Drills

These drills can also be used as good ways to end practices.

Leading Off and Getting Back W11
Purpose: To simulate a pitching situation so players learn when to leave the base on a pitched ball. This drill helps players hone their timing when leading off and getting back to the base safely.

Players line up on the first-base foul line, spacing themselves a few feet apart. The coach stands on the pitcher's mound and goes through a simulated pitching motion. Players pretend the foul line is a base. They watch the coach go through the pitching motion and get ready to lead off the bag to run to the next base. Players can lead off with a *rocker step*, where they put one foot on the front edge of the bag and keep the back foot behind the base. Players rock in a timed motion, beginning when the pitcher's arm is at the top of her motion. By the time the pitcher's arm comes down and she releases the ball, the runner has already gone. Players on the foul line can also lead off like traditional baseball players, where the player puts her left foot on the base facing the batter and leaves the base when the pitcher releases the ball.

Players then practice getting back to the bag, as they would if the batter did not hit the pitch. Players can return to the base standing up or can dive back in. In diving back, the player reaches for the back of the bag with her hands and turns her face away, toward the outfield, so she doesn't get hit by the ball or a glove.

Jog-Sprint-Jog W12
Purpose: To provide conditioning and to focus on the technique for form running.

Players go to the outfield grass on one foul line. In groups of twos or threes, players jog a third of the way across the brim (where the dirt meets the grass), sprint for a third, and then jog for the final third of the field, to the opposite foul line. Players should focus on their form running technique: knees should be straight, with feet kicking back, arms pumping, and head still. Players can build up to as many as 6 or 8 repetitions of this drill.

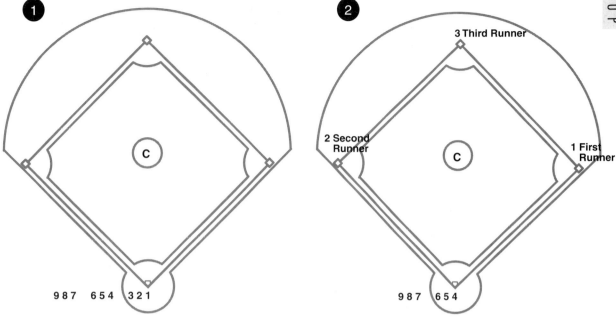

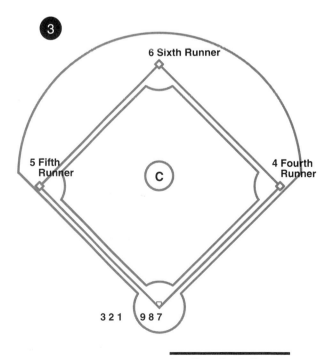

One, Three, Two Drill W13

Purpose: To teach baserunning with the whole team.

The team lines up at home plate, in groups of three. The coach, standing out on the pitcher's mound, simulates a pitch. The first player in the first group runs through first base and stays on first. The second player "hits" a triple and runs to third. The third player in the group hits a double and goes to second. They all stay on the bases and take a lead on the next simulated pitch. The next group of three players hits the same sequence, advancing the first group of players around the bases. Each group that "hits" advances the previous group around the bases so that everyone gets practice running bases and leading off.

One, Three, Two Drill

Wrist Snaps: the more snap, the better the pitch.

Drills for Pitchers

These drills are a breakdown of the entire pitching motion.

Wrist Snaps W14

Purpose: To toss the ball with a snap of the wrist. The greater the wrist snap, the greater the potential pitches with speed.

Players and their partners stand 5 feet apart. The player who is doing the wrist snaps turns sideways toward her partner, with her pitching arm straight at her side. She is not wearing a glove and holds her nonpitching arm steady just above the wrist. She cocks her throwing wrist back and then flips the softball to her partner, using only the wrist to propel the ball. The partner tosses the ball back; then the pitching partner cocks her wrist and flips the ball back again. Her hand stays behind the ball at all times. The goal is to make the ball spin as many rotations as possible. If both players are pitchers, they can alternate doing wrist snaps.

Elbow Snaps W15

Purpose: To practice a continuation of the pitching motion.

This drill is set up the same way as Wrist Snaps (see drill W14 above), with partners standing 5–10 feet apart. The partner with the ball cocks her wrist, snaps the ball, and allows her wrist *and* elbow to flex, so that she follows through, and her fingertips end up touching her shoulder and her elbow pointing toward the target.

One-Knee Arm Circles W16

Purpose: To focus on the pitcher's upper body.

The player is on one knee and makes a one-arm circle as she pitches to a target or catcher, focusing on keeping her shoulders back and her torso straight up and down as she releases the ball.

Half Strides W17

Purpose: To reinforce the motion of stepping off the rubber at the beginning of the pitch.

Players stand farther from the target than in other pitching drills—approximately 30 feet away. The drill focuses on the point in the pitch where the player pushes off the rubber, lands with both of her feet at a 45-degree angle, and is sideways to the catcher. Her pitching arm should be straight above her head, with her wrist cocked so the ball is pointing straight up at the sky. Players should start at this spot in this position and do a one-arm revolution, keeping their feet where they are but allowing them to pivot. The hips turn but the feet remain in place.

Half Strides reinforce the motion of stepping off the rubber.

Half Strides, Finish with Lower Body W18

Purpose: Putting the entire pitching motion together.

This drill begins with the same motion as Half Strides (see drill W17 above) but the pitcher's back foot pushes forward and comes up to meet her front foot just slightly after the ball is released to the catcher. Another way to describe this is that the pitcher brings her back knee into the back of her front knee.

One-Knee Double Arm Circles W19

Purpose: To develop arm speed as the pitching arm goes around.

The player swings her arm around twice, going as fast as she can and letting go of the ball on the second revolution.

Fast-Pitch with Real Softball W20

Purpose: To practice hitting in a simulated "live" pitching situation.

The coach pitches the ball to the player to give her an opportunity to practice batting in a live situation. The player can run out the hit, take turns with another player, or take a specific number of cuts.

Throw a Pitch W21
Purpose: To complete the pitching motion.

The pitcher combines all the elements of the throwing progression into a full-motion pitch from full distance.

Throw Fast Balls to the Four Corners of the Plate W22
Purpose: To work on pitching accuracy.

The pitcher throws pitches from full distance, attempting to cover all four corners of the plate. This is a drill for advanced pitchers.

Variation: The pitcher can throw to targets on a wall.

Work on Alternating Pitches W23
Purpose: To work on a variety of pitches.

Players alternate between pitching a drop ball and pitching a fast ball, or between a change-up and a fast ball. This is a drill for advanced pitchers.

Drills for Catchers

Blocking Balls in the Dirt W24
Purpose: To block balls in the dirt or low pitches so they remain in front of the catcher.

Either a partner or the coach stands approximately 15 feet away from the catcher, who is in full gear and assumes a ready catching position. Starting with softie balls, the coach throws a ball in the dirt in front of the catcher, who drops to her knees, replacing her feet with her knees and putting her glove in the space between her legs. The catcher rolls her shoulders in toward the ball and drops her chin to make an enclosed area with her body to trap the ball. She then throws the ball back to the coach, who again throws the ball in the dirt. The catcher's partner or the coach should throw many repetitions of this drill using softie balls until the catcher is comfortable and ready to use a regular softball.

Catchers Throwing to Bases W25
Purpose: To practice throwing the ball to the bases from a catching position.

Infielders should be at each of the three bases. The coach tosses the ball to the catcher with an underhand throw. She receives the ball, bringing her glove and throwing hand to her throwing-side ear and turning her body sideways as she comes up. The catcher practices throwing to the bases, throwing inside the foul line at first and third base. In her throw to second base, it is better if she throws a low, bouncing ball quickly than a high, slow, looping one.

Five-Ball Drill W26

Purpose: To give the catcher practice at fielding bunts.

The catcher goes into her crouch. The coach places five balls in front of the catcher and determines the base she should throw to. When the coach yells "Go!" the catcher pops up out of her position, surrounds the ball in the direction she wants to throw it, throws one of the balls to the designated base, runs back into position, and gets back into a crouch. As soon as she is back in this position, she pops out again and does the drill again. The catcher should repeat the drill until all five balls are gone.

Pop-Ups W27

Purpose: To practice catching pop-ups directly over the catcher's head or behind her.

The catcher goes into her crouch behind home plate. The coach stands behind her, taps her shoulder to start the drill, and throws the ball high into the air. The catcher locates the ball and catches the pop-up between the eyes and the top of the chest, not over her head where she can't see it. If she is wearing headgear that she needs to throw off to see the pop-up, she should hold onto the mask until she locates the pop-up. Then she throws the mask in the opposite direction so she doesn't trip on it.

Setup and Foot Placement on Throws W28

Purpose: To promote proper foot placement on the catcher's throws.

The catcher sets up behind the plate. The coach stands out in front of the catcher, acting like the pitcher and checking that the catcher's stance isn't lopsided. Her glove hand shouldn't be too close to her chest, and she should be relaxed. When the coach throws the ball, the catcher receives it, quickly brings it to her ear, and sets her feet in the direction she will throw. The catcher must turn sideways, with her back foot perpendicular to her target. The more quickly she sets up her feet, the more power she'll gain from her body throwing the ball, rather than her arm.

CHAPTER 10

Defensive Fundamentals: Infield Play, Outfield Play, and Team Defense

Infield Drills

Two-Knees Fielding D1

Purpose: To teach players to reach out in front of themselves to catch the ball.

Many players try to field the ball between their feet with their fingertips pointing down. This drill helps teach players to reach out with the back of their gloves touching the ground. It also teaches players to use "soft hands" when bringing the ball into their bodies.

Divide your team into partners. Both partners kneel on both knees approximately 5–7 feet apart. One player rolls a ground ball or short hop to her partner, who has her glove flat on the ground. The partner reaches out to receive the ball and then "gives" with the ball, as if receiving an egg in her glove. The receiving player should watch the ball the entire time it goes into her glove, placing her throwing hand on top of the ball. The player with the ball now rolls the ball back to her partner, who fields it in the same way. Each player fields the ball this way 10 times.

Two-Knees Fielding teaches players to reach out when fielding.

Three-Player Throwing D2

Purpose: To practice fielding, catching, and throwing quickly.

Divide your players into groups of three. Each group of players forms a triangle, approximately 10 feet apart. One player, designated the tosser, throws a grounder or line drive to the second player, who fields (catches) it and immediately throws to the third player. The third player throws it back to the tosser, who starts the play again. Players take turns tossing and fielding after every five tosses and rotate how they stand so that they practice throwing in different directions.

Variation: This drill can also be done by outfielders. Increase the distance between the tosser and receiver to an appropriate outfield depth.

Footwork on a Force-Out and Tag Play D3

Purpose: To practice tagging players at bases.

This drill works on all outs at every base; the footwork is the same. Divide your players into two groups. One group lines up at second base, and one at first. The coach and an assistant each take a group. Players at first work on footwork for a force-out; players at second work on footwork for a tag out. One at a time, players at first base start a few steps off the bag and, at a signal, run back to the bag, put the right foot (if they are right-handed) on the bag, and stretch toward the ball thrown by the coach. Players at second base should run over to the bag, take half the bag away on the side from which the runner is coming, and then sweep their glove down in front of the bag for a tag out. Ideally the ball should be thrown eye level or lower for a force-out and at knee level for a tag out. Players don't stretch until the ball has been released. Players should always leave the bag to get a bad throw and then come back to the bag.

Balls in Positions D4

Purpose: To practice fielding ground balls in the infield and outfield.

Players take their positions on the field. The coach is at the plate, hitting fungoes to players at their positions. Players either throw the ball back to home plate or work on game situations such as "one runner on base, no outs" or "two outs, runners on second and third." Switch players around so that different players get to try fielding grounders at a variety of positions.

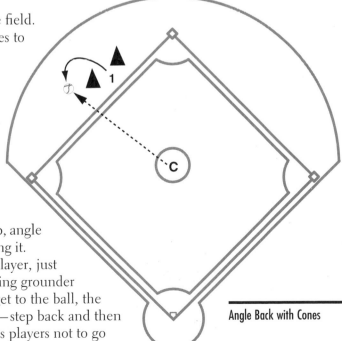

Angle Back with Cones D5

Purpose: To help players learn to drop-step, angle back, and surround the ball when fielding it.

Place a cone on either side of a player, just behind her. The coach hits a slow-moving grounder just on the other side of one cone. To get to the ball, the player must drop-step around the cone—step back and then take a step to the side. This drill teaches players not to go straight across to the ball.

Angle Back with Cones

Outfield Drills

Down and Block D6

Purpose: To practice getting down and blocking the ball to keep it in front of the body. Players can use this technique whenever no one is on base, when the field conditions are poor, or when it is critical that the ball doesn't get by the outfielders.

Players work in partners, tossing the ball to each other. The player receiving the ball surrounds the ball, drops to one knee with her shoulders square to the ball, and blocks the ball from getting past her into the outfield. She then throws the ball the same way to her partner.

Variation: The players stand in a line, and the coach rolls or hits a ball to each player in line, who fields the ball as above.

Like an Infielder D7

Purpose: To practice fielding ground balls in the outfield just like fielding grounders in the infield.

The setup is the same as Down and Block (see drill D6), but fielders practice the techniques used in Two-Knees Fielding (see drill D1 on page 98) and regular infield ground balls. Outfielders should use this technique when runners are on base, and a quick throw into the infield is necessary.

Fly Balls in Two Lines D8

Purpose: To teach players how to call for fly balls and the necessary teamwork required in catching called balls.

Players line up in two lines in the outfield, 30–40 yards apart. The coach hits a ball between the first player in each line. As soon as the ball is hit, one player needs to call for the ball; the other goes to back her up. The coach can designate one line as the center fielder (the person with precedence in calling for the ball), and the other line can always be ready to back the other player up, or the players can determine for themselves who should get the ball, as they would in a game. The player who calls for the ball should yell "Mine, mine!" and the other should get behind her to back her up.

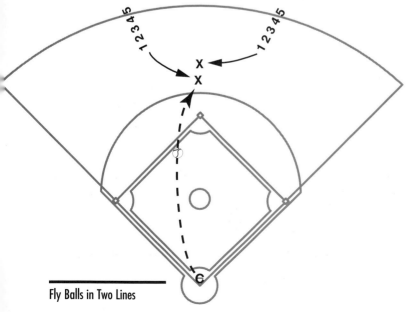

Fly Balls in Two Lines

Team Defense Drills

Infield Run for Outfield D9

Purpose: To provide a game-like situation where infielders run the bases and outfielders practice defensive plays.

Put all of your outfielders on the field, in their respective positions. All outfielders on the team should be on the field, taking turns at each position one at a time. There should be a catcher and an infielder playing at first base, second base, and shortstop. Other infield players can be base runners.

The coach sets up the play by placing base runners on certain bases and calling how many outs (for example, "Runners on second and third, one out"). Then the coach hits fungoes to the outfielders, who play the ball as in a game situation. Play the inning out or repeat the same situation for the time desired.

Outfield Run for Infield D10

Purpose: To provide a game-like situation where outfielders run the bases and infielders practice defensive plays.

This drill is identical in form to Infield Run for Outfield (see drill D9 above) but uses outfielders as base runners and requires the infielders to work on defensive plays. The coach places base runners on certain bases, calls how many outs, and then hits fungoes to the infielders, who play the ball as in a game situation. Play each inning out or repeat the same situation for the time desired.

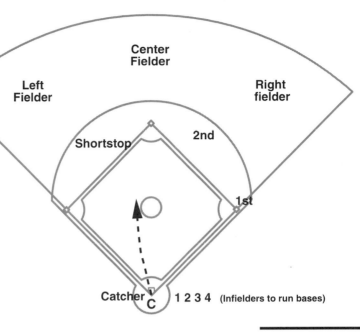

Infield Run for Outfield

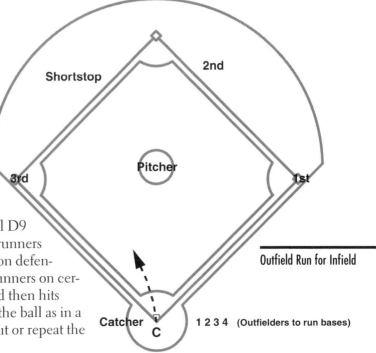

Outfield Run for Infield

DEFENSIVE FUNDAMENTALS

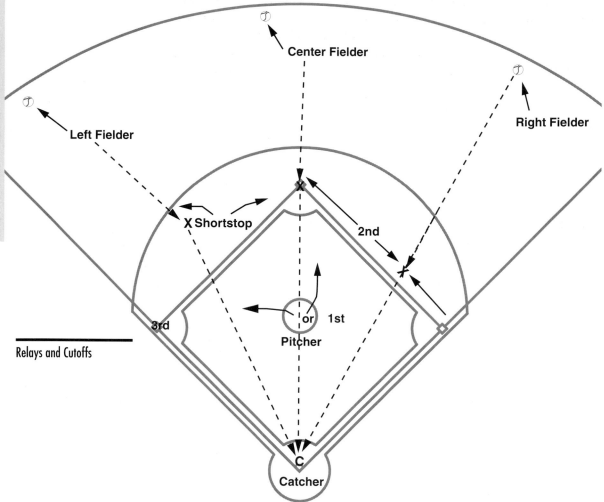

Center Fielder

Right Fielder

Left Fielder

X Shortstop

2nd

3rd

or 1st

Pitcher

Relays and Cutoffs

C

Catcher

Relays and Cutoffs (Intermediate) D11

Purpose: To help players learn how to work as a team for a relay from the outfield to home plate when a ball gets by an outfielder. The goal is to have the relay team work together in a straight line from the ball to home plate.

The whole team is out on the field in their appropriate positions. The coach places three balls in the outfield a few feet from the outfield fence, one in left field, one in right field, and one in center field. The left fielder starts this drill by running and picking up the ball at the fence. She throws to the shortstop, who has come out from her position to the edge of the infield. The catcher directs the shortstop to move to the right or left so that she lines up with home plate. The first-base player runs to the left of the pitcher's mound to take her place in the relay. If the catcher calls for the first-base player to "cut" the ball (cut off the throw to home from the shortstop), she then catches the ball and makes another play. Otherwise, the outfielder throws to the shortstop, the shortstop throws to home, and the catcher makes the play. Other players wait to see if the play will involve them. The pitcher runs in a straight line from the mound to the third-base foul line so that she can back up the play at third base or at home. The pitcher can also be used as the cutoff person instead of the first-base player.

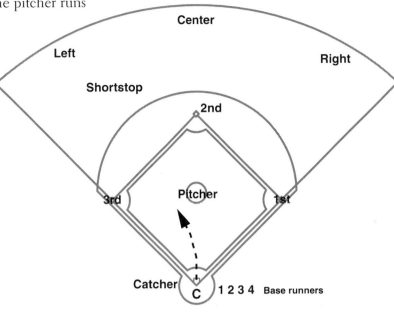

Controlled Fungo D12

Purpose: To practice game-like situations.

The whole team is on the field in their positions (with or without a pitcher). Any extra players can act as base runners, although the drill will also work without base runners. The coach sets up the play by placing runners on bases and calling the number of outs. Ghost, or pretend, runners may also be used. The coach hits fungoes from home plate, and the players (including the runners) play out the inning as if in a game situation. If there is more than one player for each position, rotate players after the players on the field have had up to five plays.

This drill is also a good way to end a practice.

Controlled Fungo

Batting Practice

Batting Drills

Single Tee Hits B1

Purpose: To work on batting technique with a stationary ball.

Players should work on swinging at high pitches (at the top of the strike zone) first. Put the ball on the batting tee set as high as it can go; then lower the height of the tee as players work from high pitches to low pitches. Players should hit into a screen when doing this drill.

The Double Tee Hits help players keep their hands inside the ball and work on maintaining a level swing.

Double Tee Hits (Intermediate or Advanced) B2

Purpose: To help players keep their hands inside the ball, hit the ball up the middle, and maintain a level swing.

Set up two batting tees with one directly in front of the other. Players swing at the ball on the back tee, keeping their hands inside the ball and swinging with a level motion. The ball on the back tee will hit the ball off the front tee. If players sweep the ball with their hands outside the ball, the first ball off the tee will miss the second one to the "pull" side. Similarly, if players uppercut or undercut their swings, the first ball won't hit the second ball. Players should hit into a screen when doing this drill.

Variation: Set up two batting tees next to each other to simulate inside and outside

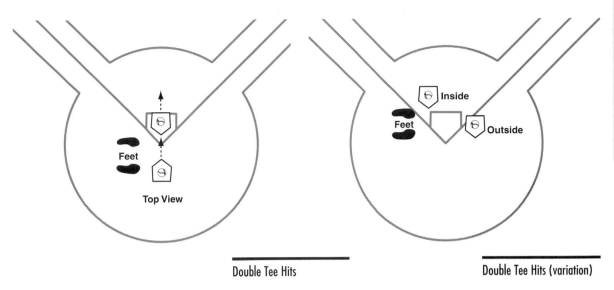

Double Tee Hits

Double Tee Hits (variation)

pitches. Players hit the ball off the first tee (the inside pitch) without hitting the second ball. This helps players learn not to hit "long" to the ball (reach for the ball with the bat). This is also an advanced drill and should be use with more experienced players.

Soft Toss B3

Purpose: To get many repetitions.

Players pair up with a partner. The batter hits into a net or out to an open space. The tosser is on one knee at a 45- to 55-degree angle to the batter, so that the batter doesn't hit the ball right at the tosser. The tosser uses an

Front Toss drills are great for hitters. If you don't have a protective screen for the tosser, use whiffle balls, as above. (See description on page 106)

underhand toss to throw the ball into the hitting area, and the batter swings, keeping in mind proper batting form. Each player should hit 10–20 balls each, and then switch places.

Front Toss B4

Purpose: To practice hitting balls from a front source.

The batter stands in the batter's box, with the protective screen approximately 15–30 feet out in front of the batter. The coach sits or stands directly behind the screen so only her arm comes out. She tosses the ball and ducks behind the screen before the batter hits the ball. Keeping a bucket of balls handy means players don't have to track down the ball after every hit. (See photo on page 105)

Variation: This drill can also be performed without a protective screen with a whiffle ball. Players can then choose partners for the drill, with one player tossing balls and the the other batting. Players then switch places. Using partners frees you up to do other coaching.

Bounce Toss B5

Purpose: To teach batters proper timing when swinging the bat.

Each player takes a turn at bat. The coach or an assistant stands at a 45-degree angle to the batter, similar to the Soft Toss setup (see drill B3). Using a softie ball, tennis ball, or other soft ball that bounces easily, bounce a ball to the player so that it bounces once to the hitting zone. The player loads up (prepares to swing) on the bounce and then follows through with her swing as the ball enters the hitting zone. Practice this drill several times per player.

Bunting Drills

Two-Player or Four-Player Toss B6

Purpose: To work on proper bunting technique.

Either two or four players can do this drill. With two players, one kneels out in front of the bunter, approximately halfway to the pitcher's mound. She throws the ball overhand to the batter. The bunter pivots around and squares her shoulders in the proper bunting position before the partner releases the ball.

With four players, a first-base player and third-base player join the first two. When the ball is bunted, the base players play out the bunt as in a game. Repeat this drill ten times, then switch the players around.

Batting Practice with a Machine B7

Purpose: To practice real-life bunting situations with a machine.

When the person who is feeding the machine presents the ball, the batter or pitcher should be pivoted around and ready.

Run and Slap (Advanced) B8

Purpose: To practice bunting, or slapping, as a way to move runners and bunt for a hit.

This drill is primarily used for the fast left-handed player, although it works for both left- and right-handed players. The player starts at the left of the batter's box, uses a cross-over step, and bunts or makes a swinging slap at the ball. Because she's so fast, she gets the ball into play and puts pressure on the defense, who throw the ball away. This is a skill for kids who can run fast and have good eye-hand coordination. This is not in lieu of learning to hit the ball properly but is an added skill for very fast left-handed players.

The player first tries this drill with a batting tee. She starts at the back of the box, takes a cross-over step, and quickly hits the ball off the tee with a downward swing. Once she can do the maneuver with the ball on a tee, she moves to soft toss, then bounce toss, and then live pitches.

One Knee, with Ball Hit off a Short Tee or Cone B9

Purpose: To teach the sequential unlocking motion of the front arm.

Players are on one knee, hitting the ball off a short tee (approximately 2 feet high) or cone. They should focus on leading with the front elbows, keeping it tucked in and down, and maintaining a level or slightly downward swing.

Whiffle Toss from Front B10

Purpose: Batting practice off a "front source;" the ball comes from the front, not from the side or from a stationary position.

The coach stands 15–25 feet in front of the batter and pitches, using an underhand motion, a whiffle ball into the pitching zone. The whiffle ball can be any size; to challenge more advanced players, try a whiffle golf ball.

APPENDIX: Umpire Signals

A. Right arm straight out front with palm outward and fingers up—signifies don't pitch and time-out. **B.** Beckoning motion with right hand at head level while facing pitcher—signifies play is to start or be resumed and simultaneously umpire calls "Play Ball." **C.** Both hands open above the head—signifies time-out, foul ball or the ball is dead immediately. **D.** Left fist extended to the side at shoulder height—signifies an infraction for which: (1) the penalty may be ignored; or (2) bases may be awarded after no further advance is possible. Illustrations are: (1) an illegal pitch, catcher obstruction, or umpire interference, and (2) fielder's illegal use of equipment in touching a ball and obstruction by a fielder. **E.; G.** Strike; Out—fist to a hammer at 90°. **F.** Right fist held above the head—signifies infield fly. **H.** Safe—extended arms, palms down. Make verbal call. **I.** Fair ball, umpire points to fair territory. **J.** Foul tip—the palms of the hands glance off each other as they pass.

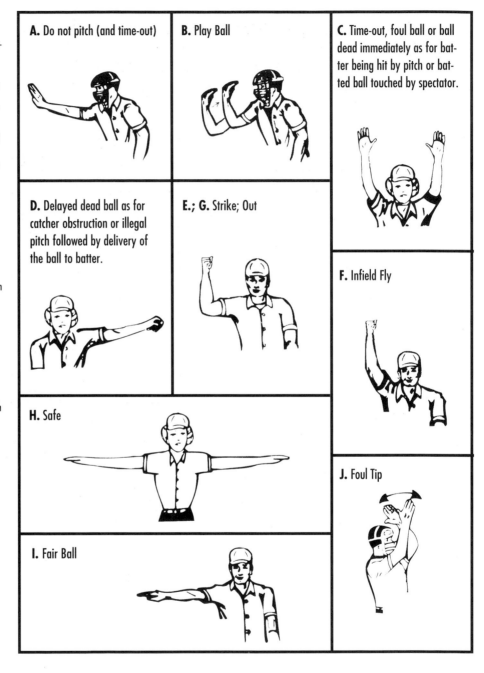

A. Do not pitch (and time-out)

B. Play Ball

C. Time-out, foul ball or ball dead immediately as for batter being hit by pitch or batted ball touched by spectator.

D. Delayed dead ball as for catcher obstruction or illegal pitch followed by delivery of the ball to batter.

E.; G. Strike; Out

F. Infield Fly

H. Safe

I. Fair Ball

J. Foul Tip

Sample Scorebook

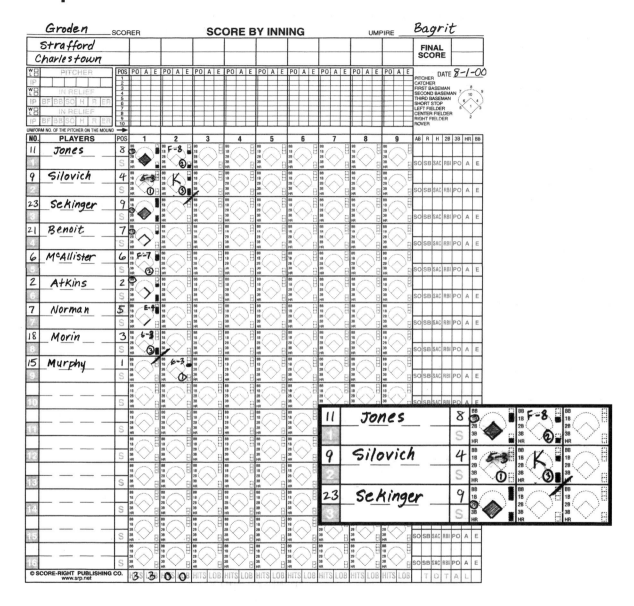

Glossary

Arm action: The movement of the throwing arm after the hands break in a throwing or pitching motion.

At bat: [statistic] A batting sequence in which a batter makes an out, gets a hit, or reaches base on an error. Being hit by a pitch, a base on balls, and a sacrifice are not recorded as official "at bats." Also, to be "at bat" is to be the batter.

Athletic stance: A balanced and ready position.

Attack the ball: While batting: taking an aggressive swing; while fielding: charging the ball aggressively.

Backhand: A catch made to the far throwing-hand side of the body with the glove positioned so that the fingers are above the thumb.

Backstop: A permanent protective screen behind home plate.

Bag: See *base*.

Ball: A pitch that is thrown out of the strike zone and at which the batter does not swing.

Base: One of 4 points that must be touched by a runner in order to score a run.

Base coach: A team member or coach who is stationed in the coach's box at first or third base.

Base hit: Any ball that is hit and results in the batter safely reaching base without an error or a fielder's choice being made on the play.

Baselines: The two lines that run from home plate through first and third base, respectively. They separate fair territory from foul and extend beyond the bases to become the right and left field lines, respectively.

Base on balls: An award of first base granted to the batter who, during the time at bat, receives 4 pitches outside of the strike zone.

Base path: The running lane for base runners.

Base runner: A player on the offense who is on base.

Bases loaded: The situation when base runners occupy first, second, and third base.

Batter: The player at bat.

Batter's box: A 3- by 7-foot area on the right and left sides of home plate in which the batter must stand when at bat.

Batting average: [statistic] The number of hits divided by the number of official at bats.

Batting tee: A piece of equipment the ball sits on. Used for batting practice.

Bent-leg slide: A sliding into a base technique in which the bottom leg is flexed under the top leg, which extends to the base.

Block technique: The catcher stops pitches that are in the dirt with her body or mitt. See also *down-and-block technique*.

Bunt: An intentionally soft hit made by the batter.

Catcher: Position 2. This fielder takes a position in back of home plate and is primarily responsible for receiving pitches.

Center fielder: Position 8. This player is positioned in the middle of the outfield.

Coach's box: A 3- by 15-foot area outside of first and third base where the coach or a player stands to coach the team when it is at bat.

Count: The number of balls and strikes thrown to a batter. Balls are acknowledged first, and strikes second.

Covering the bases: This phrase refers to a player who is responsible for plays at that base.

Crow-hop: The technique used by outfielders to organize their feet and gain momentum and power for making a throw.

Cut-off person or player: A defensive player positioned in the infield to receive throws directed to a base.

Cutoff: See *relay*.

Double play: A play in which two outs are recorded on one batted ball.

Double: A two-base hit.

Down-and-block technique: An outfield technique used to field ground balls. See also *block technique*.

Down the line: Refers to a batted ball hit near a foul line.

Drop-step: A step back and a step to the side taken by an outfielder when fielding fly balls.

Earned run average: [statistic] The number of earned runs allowed by a pitcher divided by the number of innings pitched; the product of which is multiplied by the number of innings in a game.

Error: A misplay made by a defensive player that results in a runner or runners advancing to bases that they otherwise would not have reached.

Extra innings: Innings played beyond the normal stopping point as a result of a tied score.

Fair ball: A legally batted ball that settles on or over fair territory.

Fair teritory: All arca located inside and including the baselines.

Fielder's choice: A defensive play in which the batter reaches base as a result of a defensive player opting to make a play on another base runner.

Fielding percentage: [statistic] The number of plays, putouts, or assists handled properly by a defensive player divided by the total number of chances.

First-base player: Position 3. This player is an infielder responsible for plays at first base.

Fly ball: A ball hit in the air to the outfield.

Fly out: An out made by catching the ball in the outfield.

Follow-through: A term used in both throwing, batting, and pitching to indicate the part of the throwing motion that occurs after the ball is released, or the part of the swing that occurs after the bat has gone through the contact area.

Force-out: An out made by tagging a base that must be reached by the base runner before the runner reaches the base.

Forehand: A catch made to the far glove-hand side of a player.

Form running: Proper running technique.

Foul ball: A ball that is hit into and touches foul territory.

Foul poles: The two poles that extend vertically at the points where the right and left field lines meet the outfield fence. A ball that hits a foul pole is considered to be a "fair ball."

Foul territory: All area located outside the foul lines.

Free substitution: Players may reenter the game.

Full count: 3 balls, 2 strikes on the batter.

Fungo: A ball batted in practice situations.

Glove-hand side: A ball to the glove side of a defensive player.

Grand slam: A home run hit with the bases loaded.

Ground ball: A batted ball that rolls along the ground.

Ground out: An out made on a batted ground ball.

Grounder: See *ground ball*.

Hit for the cycle: When a player hits at least one of each of the following in a single game: single, double, triple, and home run.

Hit: See *base hit*.

Hit-and-run: A planned offensive play in which a base runner steals and the batter attempts to hit the pitch on the ground behind the runner.

Hitting zone: The area in which the batter swings and attempts to hit a pitch.

Home plate: A 17-inch wide five-sided slab of whitened rubber.

Home run: A four-base hit in which the batter scores a run and is credited with an RBI.

In the gap: The space in between outfielders into which a batted ball is hit.

In the hole: The area between infielders into which a batted ball is hit.

Infielder: A defensive player who plays in the dirt area of the diamond.

Infield fly rule: A fair fly ball that can be caught by an infielder with ordinary effort, when first and second, or first, second and third bases are occupied before two are out.

Inning: A unit of play defined by two half-innings, in each of which 3 outs are recorded.

Inside pitch: A pitch thrown anywhere between the middle of the plate and the batter's body.

K: A scorer's term for a strikeout.

Launch position: The position reached during the batter's swing as the stride foot lands (and weight is transferred or "loaded" to the back foot) and just before the bat is accelerated forward toward the pitch.

Left fielder: Position 7. This player is an outfielder.

Line drive: A hard-hit batted ball that goes a distance on a horizontal plane.

Mitt: A glove used by a catcher or first-base player.

On deck: The position of the next player on the offense to bat.

On-deck circle: The area in which the on-deck batter warms up.

Out: A declaration by the umpire that a player who is trying for a base is not entitled to that base.

Outfielder: A defensive player who is positioned beyond the infield dirt. There are three outfield positions: left field, center field, and right field.

Outside pitch: A pitch thrown anywhere from the middle of the plate out away from the batter's position.

Passed ball: A pitch that gets past the catcher and is ruled the fault of the catcher.

Pinch hitter: A substitute player who bats for a player listed in the lineup.

Pinch runner: A substitute player who runs for a player who has reached base.

Pitcher: Position 1. The fielder designated to deliver the pitch to the batter.

Pitcher's circle: The circle (8-foot radius) around the pitcher's rubber.

Pitcher's rubber: A rectangular whitened rubber slab set in the ground from which the pitcher must be in contact at the start of the pitching motion.

Pocket of the glove: The inner portion of a softball glove.

Pop fly: A fly ball hit high and short over the infield or short outfield.

Relay: A defensive play in which an outfielder throws the ball to an infielder who, in turn, throws the ball to a teammate covering a base.

Relief pitcher: A player who enters the game to replace the current pitcher.

Replacing your feet: The technique used by infielders to gain momentum and quickly get their feet into a good throwing position after fielding a ground ball.

Right fielder: Position 9. This player is an outfielder.

Rip: A hard hit ball.

Run: A unit (score) awarded to the team on the offense when a runner legally advances to home plate.

Run and slap: Term to describe a batter who from the left side of the plate slaps at the ball to get it into play on the ground. Also referred to as a "slapper."

Runs batted in (RBI): Credited to a batter when a runner scores because of the batter's action (there are a few exceptions to this).

Sacrifice bunt: A batter bunts the pitch so as to advance a base runner.

Sacrifice fly: A batted fly ball that is caught for an out but that allows a runner at third base to tag up and score.

Safe: A declaration by the umpire that a runner is entitled to a base because she reached it before being put out.

Scoring position: Runners are at second or third base.

Second-base player: Position 4. This infielder is positioned to the right of the second-base bag.

Shortstop: Position 6. This infielder is positioned between second and third base.

Sidearm: A throwing motion in which the throwing arm is horizontal to the ground.

Single: A one-base hit.

Soft hands: A fielder who rhythmically funnels the ball into the body.

Softie balls: A regulation-size softball made out of soft material.

Stealing: The act of advancing one base after the pitcher has released the ball to the batter.

Strike: A pitch that is entered in the strike zone but not swung at, or a pitch at which the batter swings and misses or fouls off.

Strikeout: An out that is the result of three strikes being called, or when a batter swings and misses the third strike. Also called a *K*.

Strike zone: The area over home plate from the batter's kneecaps to directly below the batter's armpits when the batter assumes a natural stance.

Tag out: The act of a fielder tagging a base runner, or a base with the ball securely in the hand of glove.

Tag up: The act of a base runner returning to touch a base after a fly ball is caught. The runner may then attempt to advance to the next base.

Take: The batter does not swing at a pitch.

T-ball: A simulation game when the ball to be hit is placed on a tee rather than pitched.

Texas leaguer: A poorly hit fly ball that lands out of reach of an infielder and in front of outfielders. These hits are often called flares or bloop hits.

Third-base player: Position 5. This player is positioned near the third-base bag.

Triple play: A play in which three outs are recorded on one batted ball.

Triple: A three-base hit.

Umpire: The ruling official in a softball game.

Uppercut: An upward swing at a ball.

Up the middle: The area in between the shortstop and second-base player.

Walk: See *base on balls*.

Wild pitch: A pitch thrown to a location where the catcher cannot catch it.

Windmill: The most common motion used by fast-pitch pitchers.

Resources

Associations and Organizations

Amateur Softball Association
2801 NE 50th Street
Oklahoma City OK 73111
800-277-0071
www.softball.org
The national governing body of softball in the United States, the ASA establishes uniform rules and regulations for the game, sponsors tournaments at state, regional, and national levels, and offers education programs for coaches and umpires. They also sponsor a Junior Olympic Softball program for boys and girls. Their website includes information on videos, rule books, and manuals for players, coaches, and umpires.

American Sport Education Program
www.asep.com
800-747-5698
This organization offers educational courses and resources for coaches, directors, and parents to make sports safer, more enjoyable, and valuable for children and young adults. It also publishes books on coaching youth sports, including softball.

Little League Baseball, Inc.
Little League Baseball International Headquarters
P.O. Box 3485
Williamsport PA 17701
570-326-1921
Fax: 570-322-2376
www.littleleague.org
Little League Baseball offers Little League Softball programs in which girls and boys ages 5–18 participate. It offers a full range of tournament play, including a Little League Softball World Series.

National Alliance for Youth Sports
2050 Vista Parkway
West Palm Beach FL 33411
561-684-1141 or 800-729-2057
Fax: 561-684-2546
www.nays.org
This organization sponsors nine national programs that educate volunteer coaches, parents, youth sport program administrators, and officials about their roles and responsibilities. Their website provides information on these education programs, including: PAYS (Parents Association for Youth Sports); NYSCA (National Youth Sports Coaches Association); NYSOA (National Youth Sports Officials Association); and the Academy for Youth Sports Administrators.

National Fastpitch Coaches Association
409 Vandiver Drive, Suite 5-202
Columbia MO 65202
573-875-3033
Fax: 573-875-2924
E-mail: nfca@nfca.org
www.nfca.org
The NFCA is the professional growth organization for fast-pitch softball coaches from all competitive levels. Members receive the organization's newspaper, discounts on softball videos, books, and other merchandise. It sponsors scholar-athlete awards for high school and college players.

National Federation of State High School Associations
P.O. Box 690
Indianapolis IN 46206
317-972-6900
800-776-3462 (to order rule books)
Fax: 317-822-5700
www.nfhs.org
Publishes rule books for high school sports (including softball), case books (which supplement rule books), and officials' manuals.

National Youth Sports Safety Foundation (NYSSF)
333 Longwood Avenue, Suite 202
Boston MA 02115
617-277-1171
Fax: 617-277-2278
E-mail: NYSSF@aol.com
www.nyssf.org
NYSSF is a nonprofit educational organization whose goal is to reduce the risks of sports injury to young people.

North American Youth Sports Institute (NAYSI)

4985 Oak Garden Drive
Kernersville NC 27284-9520
336-784-4926 or 800-767-4916
Fax: 336-784-5546
www.naysi.com
NAYSI's website features information and resources to help teachers, coaches, and other youth leaders, including parents, interact more effectively with children around sports. It includes a resource section that lists books on sports and coaching, as well as two interactive sections where browsers can submit questions on fitness, recreation, and sports. The website's newsletter, Sport Scene, focuses on youth programs.

Women's Sports Foundation

Eisenhower Park
East Meadow NY 11554
800-227-3988
E-mail: wosport@aol.com
www.WomenSportsFoundation.
    org
The Women's Sports Foundation is a charitable educational organization dedicated to increasing the participation of girls and women in sports and fitness and creating an educated public that supports gender equity in sport.

Websites and Electronic Newsletters

Adapted Physical Education

http://pe.central.vt.edu/
E-mail: pec@vt.edu
This section of PE Central offers information to help teachers of physically challenged students. The site suggests many ways to modify sports and activities to make them accessible to all students.

ASA Properties

www.officialgear.com
800-654-8337
This site, sponsored by the Amateur Softball Association, offers softball clothing, accessories, and umpire gear.

Coaching Youth Sports

www.tandl.vt.edu/rstratto/CYS
Virginia Tech's Health and Physical Education program sponsors this website, which provides coaches, athletes, and parents with general, rather than sport-specific, information about skills for youth. The site also allows browsers to submit questions.

PE Central

http://pe.central.vt.edu
This website for physical education teachers, students, and parents is designed to provide the most current information on appropriate physical education programs, helping young people on their way to a lifetime of physical fitness and health.

PONY (Protect Our Nation's Youth)

www.pony.org
The PONY Girls Softball program provides rules and tournament play for fast-pitch and slow-pitch softball. Diamond sizes are tailored to the physical ability of the players. This website provides suggested specifications for softball playing fields for various age groups.

Sports Parents

www.sportsparents.com
Sports Parents provides a variety of articles from the magazine *Sports Parents*, a supplement to *Sports Illustrated for Kids*. Topics include coaching, sportsmanship, nutrition and fitness, equipment, sports medicine and safety, and finance and travel. A parents' tips section covers issues such as winning and losing, sibling rivalry, helping a child cope with frustration, and self-esteem.

Youth Sports Network

www.ysn.com
Youth Sports Network is a multifaceted site with a featured sport of the week, news stories about youth sports, and a directory of sports camps. An instructional page covering soccer, basketball, baseball, and softball offers tips and ideas for both players and coaches. The site also offers information on exercise, nutrition, and first aid.

Index

Page numbers in **bold** refer to pages with illustrations. The glossary and resources have not been indexed.

Acknowledgments

I wish to thank my two assistant coaches, Kim McKeon and Julie Hudson, for their commitment, work ethic, loyalty, and most importantly, their friendship.

About the Author

Jacquie Joseph has a passion for developing student-athletes who are successful on the field, in the classroom, and in the community. Those values are at the core of her softball program at Michigan State University.

Since becoming head softball coach at MSU in 1993–94, she has guided the Spartans to a record of 232–174 and two NCAA appearances. In addition, her players have earned All-America and All-Big Ten honors numerous times.

Joseph's coaching talents have been recognized on a national level as well. In June 1997, she served as co-coach of the West team at the U.S. Softball Women's National Team Festival and as an assistant coach for the U.S team that won a gold medal at the Pan-Am Qualifier in Medellín, Colombia. She has served on the board of directors of the National Fastpitch Coaches Association for the past nine years, four years as their president.

Before coaching at MSU, Joseph spent five years as the head coach at Bowling Green University. In 1992, the Falcons finished with a 34–18 record, capturing the Mid American Conference title and advancing to the NCAA regionals. She was also an assistant coach at Indiana University for one year and at her alma mater, Central Michigan State University, for two years.

Joseph is a veteran clinician and the author of *Defensive Softball Drills*, as well as several instructional videos.

Look for these other Baffled Parent's Guides by Ragged Mountain Press

The Baffled Parent's Guide to Coaching Youth Baseball,
    by Bill Thurston

The Baffled Parent's Guide to Coaching Youth Basketball,
    by David G. Faucher

The Baffled Parent's Guide to Coaching Youth Football,
    by Paul Pasqualoni

The Baffled Parent's Guide to Teaching Kids Golf,
    by Bernadette Moore

The Baffled Parent's Guide to Coaching Youth Soccer,
    by Bobby Clark